Don't Kill the Drunken Sailor
By J.L.Henry

Chapter 1

Here There Be Monsters

A violent summer storm welcomed me to New Cayenne. Every drop exploded on impact like a cannonball of warm water. The air was heavy with the dizzying smell of the sea and the dirty wet pavement. Palm trees were being bullied by the violent winds, and the houses by the harbor seemed to bend like retirees looking for their canes.

An old cab was waiting for me at the end of the pier. It was a few nails short of being a proper carriage, but it seemed to hold together. Its two horses and driver were as drenched as I was.

"You're that Charles Gates person?" he asked while eyeing me with interest.

"At your service."

"The new constable?"

"So it seems."

He grunted.

"I'm Saul. Would you mind doing some investigation work while I drive you to your place?"

I sighed. I was exhausted, but needed to enter this town with a good impression.

I looked around as the last passengers left the docks, running away from the rain, then nodded.

"With pleasure, Saul".

"Hop in."

Being of an above-average build in height as well as in weight, I tried to sit down on the wobbly carriage as carefully as possible. But we kicked off before I was fully seated, and I almost sprawled backwards into the seat. Thankfully, our vehicle survived.

The streets' cobblestones felt as if they were at war with our wheels. Each bump shook my bones to their very soul.

"Apologies, M'lord, the road is a bit rough," said the chauffeur.

"It's all right, I'm just glad to finally be on solid ground."

"Quite solid indeed! This pavement is so craggy, it can either make a man, or break one."

"So what's your story, Saul?"

He slowed the cab down, leaned towards me, and raised an eyebrow.

"Do you believe in monsters, mister Gates?"

I hesitated, afraid of where this was going.

"In my line of work, I only deal with the kind that walks on two feet and that keeps my job running," I deflected.

"No, I was thinking more about... Krakens."

So Saul was the sort of chap to believe in such things. I did my best to keep a neutral face. The rain helped.

"You see," he continued, "I'm a bit of an adventurer myself, having been a pirate my whole life, and by God have I seen some strange things in my days!"

"I can only imagine."

"Oh, try as you may, you won't even get close. And yet, I feel stumped."

2

"Stumped?"

"Completely. You see, I've devised an ingenious device, half boat, half fishing net, fully independent. I send it out in the evening, and it comes back in the morning, generally filled to the brim with fish. Every day, for about five years now. Day in, and day out."

"Impressive."

"I must humbly agree with you. However, lately, it hasn't been coming back."

"Is that so?"

"On my father's grave, unless the bugger is still alive, I wouldn't know."

We went over a cobblestone that had started to break free from its days of servitude as part of the pavement. It almost sent me overboard. Saul, unfazed, carried on with his story.

"At first, I blamed it on a typical sea incident. Made a new one, and sent it out. But once again," he spat, "it never came back. So I did some constable work of my own."

"So you did. How did it go?"

"Not so well."

"You don't say?"

"I almost died. But I found something."

He looked around, as if there was the slightest chance anyone had stayed out in that dreadful weather to eavesdrop on a couple of no ones.

"It was night. Pitch black. I went out, then started going around the island."

"Why at night? Wouldn't the day have made it easier?"

"My devices were taken at night, so I had to respect the proper time of crime."

"How so very clever of you."

"Wait, it gets better."

"I can imagine."

"At one point, I felt that something wasn't right."

Yes, you being in the middle of the Ocean at night.

"It was all dark, but somewhere in front of me, it was darker. And huge."

He made eye contact with me, and stuck with it so intently that I was afraid we'd miss a turn and end up in someone's living room.

"And, what did it turn out to be?" I finally gave in and asked.

"I don't know. I sensed imminent danger, turned around, and went back to the harbor."

"In that darkness?"

"Mister Gates, I am an old sailor. I could find my way to the Cape of Good Hope blindfolded. But I also know which dangers to thwart, and which ones to run away from."

"And you believe it may have been a kraken?"

"I don't believe in krakens."

"But didn't you say…"

"I don't know what I saw. All I know is I'm certain that's what took my fishing device."

He fell silent, and went back to focusing on the road. I let out a discreet sigh of relief.

"So what do you think?" he finally asked.

"Could it have been a reef? Your device goes out, gets heavy with fish. An undertow catches it unawares, and crashes it into that reef?"

"Good guess, but I had already thought of it. And this was no reef. I know the waters around this island like the veins on the back of my hand. Not a reef."

"Could it have been another ship?"

4

"What ship stays at large without a single light?"

I almost replied "a ghost ship", but had enough common sense to keep that one for myself.

"I guess I'll have to look into it."

"I sure hope you do."

The trip lasted less than a half hour. We went through the city, from the middle-class neighborhoods of the Harbor District, through the posh mansions of Moon Street, until we got to our destination, deep into the heart of the poorer part of the city.

"There you go sir, Marvin's Reach."

That was the name of my office. I saw a two-story house, old and exhausted beyond any hope of repair.

Saul raised an eyebrow at me, hinting at a tip. I slipped my last coin in his palm as I left the cab.

~

I sloshed my way to the door.

I may as well have swum all the way from Bristol. My luggage wasn't faring much better.

The second I stepped inside, the skies cleared up, and I swear a Toucan or some other noisy Caribbean bird started laughing at me. From the inside, the place didn't look so bad. Its two stories seemed intent on becoming one, and you could still see the rusted iron bars on the windows. Nevertheless, it had potential.

"With some curtains and a splash of paint, this place could become a cozy little love nest," I said to the bird.

"Mister Gates?" asked a feminine voice coming from a room to my right.

I walked in, and saw a middle-aged lady sitting behind a desk.

"So there is still some life in here," I told her.

She had ash-blond hair tied in a simple bun, glasses, and the look of a person tired of kicking butt for a living.

"I am indeed Charles Gates, and I suppose you are the notary public, the highly praised Selena Montgomery?"

She smiled wryly.

"You are as good as they say, master Gates."

"Just Charles."

She eyed me from my shoes all the way up to my head, apparently deciding not to comment on my size.

"Well I guess I'll be just Selena, then, although people around here call me 'sir'."

"Just Selena sounds just fine. So, how's business on this side of the ocean?"

"Well to start with, we tend to prefer dry clothes around here..." she said, glancing at my attire.

"Sorry, Milady, I lost a battle with the elements. They seem to be quite feisty around here, don't they?"

"That light shower? I'm sorry to say that you haven't seen anything yet."

She stood up and started pacing, her thick boot heels sending dangerous tremors through the whole building.

"Anyway, we're not here to talk about the weather. I must tell you that you've been appointed at a very..."

She seemed to hum the atmosphere to find the correct word.

"Shifty time. And as you may have learned on the sea, 'shifty' doesn't rhyme well with oacy."

"Rhymes with a much cruder word if you ask me..."

"The mayor is stepping down, and as we speak, he is introducing his replacement to our little town."

"Jack Boots is leaving? Why, and who's the happy new mayor?"

"Bartholomew James, a highly skilled lawyer from Liverpool."

"Sounds like you're thrilled at the prospect."

"What I feel like is irrelevant. Just keep in mind that change is always cause for some turmoil. Especially that the city's affairs have been doing poorly lately, with our reputation of lawlessness..."

"Which is why you hired me."

"Exactly. Law enforcement, *proper* law enforcement, would clean up our image and get us back in business."

"And as for the *why*?"

She raised an eyebrow.

"Why is Mayor Boots leaving?" I specified.

"None of my business. Probably found a better place to grow old and die."

She turned to face me.

"Now before I leave, your very first case is waiting in your office. A kidnapping. And to assist you, your partner should be coming right this... Instant!"

The second you are aware of a trap, it's already too late. I recognized the sound of shackles and chains amidst the hubbub of the street and the nearby jungle.

A man walked in, manhandled by two others who bore the universal attitude of guards on duty.

The prisoner was tall, scrawny, unshaven, and his eyes held the world in contempt. The other two... Well they just looked like guards doing their job, thinking of the next rum and pipe break.

"Mister Gates, I mean Charles, this is Nathaniel, your new partner."

"I had hoped for someone more on the good side of the law."

"I see why you would think that, but he's been sentenced as the next assistant constable, for community service."

"He's been sentenced… As in, this is his punishment? You've assigned a criminal as my partner?"

"I prefer the word 'repentant' in his case, don't you think, Nathaniel?"

The shackled man, who seemed to oscillate between his twenties and his forties, shot her a look that would have made a grown sailor blush.

"If you say so, sir," he said, dropping the last word with as little respect as possible. He then looked me up and down. "With all due respect, sir, is that wet thing the person I'm supposed to assist?"

She smiled, and headed for the door.

"Very well gentlemen, now that my job here is done, I'll leave you to yours. And welcome to New Cayenne, *just* Charles."

As she left, the guards started stirring a key in Nathaniel's shackles.

"Clockwise, Ed," said one of them, "you gotta turn it clockwise, or else, you may as well be wiping yourself with a dirty towel."

The other guard, struck by the depth of such a top-tier philosophical statement, twisted the key in every possible direction except the right one, having never paid attention to a clock.

"What if we tried this?" suggested Nathaniel, while inserting his index in the keyhole.

A loud click resonated through the room. The guards stared at him, then at each other, shrugged it off and left with barely a salute in my diroction.

"So," he said without looking at me, "do you plan on changing your clothes, or is that how you do things in...?"

8

"Bristol. No, we also enjoy dry clothes back home. Why are you still here?"

He blinked.

"I'm sorry, I'm afraid I'm not following."

The contrast between his well-mannered words and his blunt stare was almost painful.

"You don't want to be here. You hate being here. I'm not even sure *I* want you to be here. But yet, here you are, unshackled, making a mockery of this whole situation."

"Oh we can agree on that, I don't want to be here. And I will escape as soon as it won't mean certain death to me. You see, the reason I'm under arrest is that half the pirate population of this island wants me six feet under for some disagreements."

"What kind of disagreements?"

"The usual kind, about gold, and whose pockets it should be in."

"And the other half?"

"They just want me dead. As you may have noticed with your cunning skills, I'm not the likeable type. At least to them."

During his little speech, he had imperceptibly inched towards the desk. Before I had the time to do anything, he sat on it with the ease of a spoiled teenage prince in his royal bedroom.

"You do have an unconventional charm," I replied.

"There we go, I'm having the same effect on you. Don't worry, I won't linger for long."

"I certainly wouldn't want you to feel unwanted around here."

"I appreciate the sense of humour, one good point for you. Just know that when I vanish, it will happen when all the blame that lies on my shoulders will have shifted to yours."

I wrung one of my sleeves. A little waterfall splattered on the floor.

"And why would you tell me your plans?"

"Because a good magician always empties his pockets before the act. Makes it look like actual magic."

I suddenly felt tired, and my body ached for dry clothes.

"So, are you going to see your new case?" he asked.

I had completely forgotten about it.

"I suppose they can wait until I make myself more comfortable."

"Ah, you don't know much about pirates."

"Enlighten me."

Nathaniel sat down behind the desk, and put his feet up.

"You see, they're not the patient type, so to speak."

"Oh dear, am I at risk of losing a client to the competition? Many other constables out there on the island?"

"Not exactly. They may just take the matter in their own hands, and you'd end up with a few more corpses than you had started with."

I sighed.

"Very well, I guess the dry clothes can wait."

I went to the waiting room, and saw the men.

They sat at opposite ends of a bench. I made a mental note to add some furniture to make the room look more like a room, and less like a cell.

One wore some kind of beret that seemed to have lost its exact shape quite a while ago. As well as its color. It hid half his face, letting us see only one eye that glared at the other man.

Man number two was on the richer side of the wardrobe.

He had a royal blue hat that could protect the whole body from the sun. It bore the feather of a bird big enough to feed a family of eight for at least a week.

He had silk ruffles and frills growing out of every nook and cranny of his coat, white tights on his calves, and high heeled shoes.

He also wore a wig. A wig that tried to outperform the rest of the attire, with a lot of brown waves that must have involved a squadron of curlers.

He did however have a point in common with the first man: a hateful stare, aimed at the other.

"Good morning, gentlemen," I started, hoping to break some of the ice.

I instantly regretted it.

All three venomous eyes turned on me, making me feel a chill on top of being wet.

Luckily, a good idea hit me.

"My name is Charles Gates, and my assistant Nathaniel will now register your names and occupations. Once you are done, I will be waiting for you in my office."

I glanced at Nathaniel, who replied with a flawless poker face. I took that as a yes.

I hurried into what I thought was my office, and without taking the time to think, opened my suitcase, found dry clothes, threw the wet ones out the window, changed, and sat at my desk.

Meanwhile, the voice level in the other room had gone from loud to downright shouting. Even though I was glad that Nathaniel had to deal with it instead of me, I knew I couldn't let the situation fester any longer.

Before I could call them in, my door flew open and banged loudly on the wall, drastically shortening the hinges' life expectancy.

"Master Gates," started the high maintenance man, "I demand that-"

"That poor excuse of a sailor should be hung with his guts coming out from where the sun doesn't…" interrupted the other, and once again, everyone was shouting at the same time.

Nathaniel stood in the doorway, his poker face teetering on the edge of sarcasm.

"Gentlemen, gentlemen, *please*!" I shouted. "I cannot be of any help in these conditions. Do have a seat, and have the common courtesy of waiting for your turn to speak!"

"Very well," said the wig, looking around. "Are we expected to sit on the floor?"

To my horror, I realized the room was barely more furnished than the first one, if you could call my wobbly desk furniture.

"Or do you want us to hang outside in the trees like your wet clothes?" asked the limp beret with half his smile showing.

I did not need to turn around to know that my operation "quick wardrobe change" had taken a sharp turn to the south, stripping me of my last shred of authority.

I closed my eyes, stood up, and breathed in until my chest was fully expanded. They took a step back.

"Listen you two, I just got here. Wait, not done yet, still talking," I quickly added, sensing an imminent interruption. "I have spent the last eight weeks dealing with storms, nausea, scurvy, bad rum, flat beer, soggy cookies and leathery meat. Instead of arriving to a warm and welcoming home, I was drenched by my very first tropical storm. I can't even begin to tell you how ready I am to bite someone's head off. Therefore, if you were planning on getting any semblance of justice for your little disagreement, I highly suggest you show some cooperation."

By the end of my little speech, I wasn't shouting, I was bellowing. They seemed more surprised than tamed, but at that point, I couldn't be picky.

"You'll take turns so I can make some sense of this."

I put my hands on the desk, and leaned in slightly. Just not too much, for fear of having the old thing collapse under my weight. I looked at Beret Boy.
"You start."
They both looked shocked. Fancy Wig because he hadn't been given firstsies in spite of his expensive clothing, and Beret Boy because it must have been a first for him.
Nathaniel chimed in.
"This is Solomon Quickbit, retired sailor on the Afternoon Glory, which used to belong to the late captain Malcolm."
"Very well, Solomon Quickbit, what ails you?"
He had lost all the arrogance he usually got from being treated as the underdog.
"Well, mister Gates sir, it's that this man here, I believe, how can I put it... I strongly believe that he has killed his wife."
Fancy Wig seemed to have swallowed a bucketful of cayenne pepper.
"Why you little barnacle turd, I won't let..."
"Hold on mister..." I looked at Nathaniel.
"Admiral Godefroy Winchester, retired from the royal navy," he filled me in.
"Admiral Winchester, I need you to wait for your turn. Mister Quickbit, do you have any proof to support your claims?"
"I bloody well do! He hates my guts as well as hers, especially since she started fancying me over him!"
The admiral's skin tone was turning into an unhealthy type of red, so I decided Quickbit's time was over.
"Very well, very well. Admiral Winchester? I suppose your version of the story doesn't corroborate mister Quickbit's?"

His bulging eyes seemed to secrete smoke, but as he was about to explode, guts and all, he deflated. He then took a slow, deep breath, and gained back his composure.

"Mister Gates," he hissed, "I cannot begin to tell you how wrong this travesty of an investigation is, but let me start with the truth."

"And nothing but?" I tried.

"I accuse this man of having kidnapped my wife, after drugging her with an elixir from that horrible voodoo couple down Creole Street."

"And I suppose your evidence is also compelling?"

He paused, then looked at me.

"Would it be too much to ask for a private audience?" he asked.

"Once we're done here."

He pinched his lips.

"You were going to tell me about the evidence?" I asked with a good dose of insolence.

"Later, once we are done here."

There was so much poison in his tone that I felt ill.

"Very well. So, at the end of the day, you're both here for a missing person, caring more about blaming it on each other than what may have actually happened to her."

I could hear them reconsidering their attitude.

"No, of course not, I'm worried sick about her."

"I wouldn't forgive myself if anything…"

"She's the apple of my eye…"

"Thank you gentlemen, that'll be enough," I interrupted. "You are of course required to remain within the town limits until the end of this case."

"So, you're not going to arrest one of us straight away?" asked Quickbit.

14

"I need a culprit to arrest, and a mere accusation does not make one guilty, mister Quickbit."

His eye did a quick back and forth. Things obviously hadn't gone the way he had expected.

"And how soon shall you begin your search?" asked Winchester. "My wife's life is at stake after all."

"Aren't you the one who thinks she was kidnapped?" I replied.

"Yes... But on this island, between kidnapping and killing, there's barely a nuance."

"See? See? I told you he killed her! He knows! He *knows*! That's a, er, confusion right there!"

"You mean a confession, you twit," said Winchester, "and if someone darnedly looks like a suspect, it's the no-good scallywag who tried to break a family apart!"

I grew alarmingly aware that these two were armed, and that their hands were inching towards their belts.

"That's enough!" I growled. "I need you two to go home and stay there… Anyone who disobeys will be seen as a prime suspect, and if one of you two turns up dead, may God help the other!"

It was then that I realized how thin this house's walls were, and how loud my voice had gotten. A few heads were peering in from the windows, probably curious to see if this was going to evolve into something *really* interesting.

It was my turn to calm down.

"Thank you gentlemen."

I sat.

Solomon Quickbit simply left, seemingly used to that kind of dismissal. Winchester, on the other hand, just stood there, staring at Nathaniel and the onlookers. They sensed the tone, and decided to leave as well.

The man was a natural at making others feel unwanted.
"Yes, mister Winchester?" I asked him, purposely leaving his title out.
"Master Gates, I hope you are aware of all the ins and outs of this affair."
"Working on them as we speak."
"No. You were hired to bring some semblance of justice on this island. But I suggest you get acquainted with who brought you here, so that you know *whose* justice you are to uphold."
"Right. I wouldn't be detecting a hint of threat, would I, mister Winchester?"
"When a man is about to take a dip in a shark-infested pool, you don't call warning him a threat."
"No, unless it's the shark who's warning me."
He gave me a very cold stare full of promises, and walked out.
Nathaniel loomed in through the door.
"It's so exciting to see you making new friends on your first day!"
"That bad?"
"I would tell you to run to the harbor to catch your boat before it sails back to Bristol, but I still need you to get out of the town's debt."
"I appreciate the selflessness."
"Keep it up, and you'll have no self left to worry about. So what's next on the menu?"
I closed my eyes, and rubbed my nose.
"That voodoo couple on..."
I waved a hand in the air.
"Creole Street?" he helped.
"Yes, thank you."

Chapter 2
Bully in the Alley

"Their actual names are Reine and Félix, by the way," said Nathaniel, as we walked down the streets that led to the docks.

I was daydreaming about having a pint at The Hatchet Inn in Bristol, and his comment caught me off guard. Little did I know that later that day, I would have more to drink than I had bargained for.

"Who now?"

"The 'voodoo couple', as admiral Winchester put it. I'm sure they'd prefer being called by their actual names."

"Reine and Félix. Got it. French?"

"In a way..."

"The names are French."

"Given by their very French slave master."

"I see. They were given their freedom, and they moved here."

"It's more like they took their freedom with their own hands, and found refuge here."

"New Cayenne is a haven against slavery?"

"I wouldn't go that far, knowing that many here were in the slave trade. But for now, it is generally frowned upon."

Some of the streets we went through were so narrow I could have touched both sides just by stretching out my arms. I also quickly learned to avoid the bucket loads of filthy water that were randomly thrown out of windows.

"Come to think of it, I see how pirates would oppose slavery," I said. "I mean, after all, your very existence comes from breaking free from the rich and powerful."

"Unless one manages to *become* rich and powerful. There are some who itch to go back to the old ways."

"Like Winchester?"

"Like Winchester. He'd be one of them all right."

The smell of the sea had become quite strong. Seagulls appeared more frequently, and in hungry mobs.

"Here we are," he said.

We came out of a tiny, sinuous alleyway, and out into a wide succession of shops, street vendors, jugglers and other types of entertainers.

"The marketplace," I observed.

"Can't hide anything from our great policeman, can we?"

He led the way into a small entrance that turned out to be an alley: Creole Street. We went up a flight of stairs against the side of a two-story building. There was a door, with the carving of a cross strangled by a snake.

"Apothecaries! Not quite what I imagined when he said voodoo."

"The quip is meant to get at them."

"Right. Not the nicest man in the world, this Admiral?"

"Let's say there is room for improvement. Lots of room."

He looked at me, and almost heard me thinking.

"But as much as anyone would enjoy seeing him behind bars, I don't think he can be a killer."

"Not even a kidnapper?"

Nathaniel snorted.

"Kidnap his wife? Him and what army?"

He knocked on the door.

"We can talk later. People get nervous when strangers chat on their doormat."

The door opened almost instantly.

I saw a little woman. She had the white hair and the demeanor that comfortably settle in with the years.

"Who is it?" asked a deep voice from somewhere inside.

"If you care so much to know, why didn't *you* answer the door?" she said.

"Hello, my name is Charles Gates, and this is my assistant Nathaniel. We are the New Cayenne Law Enforcement Unit."

"The N.C.L.E.U.?" whispered Nathaniel. "There *has* to be something better."

"Law enforcement?" asked the lady. "Since when do we enforce the law around here?"

"As of today it seems," I answered.

"Well, sorry to disappoint you, but even in this lawless place, we've managed to remain outstanding citizens. Good day!"

The door slammed so close to my face that my nose tingled.

I knocked again.

"If you're trying to get us back on the continent to our old profession," boomed the man's voice, "I hope you came heavily armed."

"No sir," I said, "it's about the disappearance of Lady Winchester."

"Well what about it?" I heard the woman's voice through the door.

"If you could let us in, we just need some information. Nothing else, I promise."

Nathaniel raised his eyebrow at me.

A silent back and forth went on inside.

"All right," she said, while opening slowly. "But the second you do something unorthodox, you'll regret it."

"And we thank you for your cooperation," I said while stepping in.

It was a little shop, full of dark corners.

Uneven rows filled with pots and vials covered the walls, and behind a heavy wooden counter, stood a short man with salt and pepper hair. His frown brought out all his wrinkles.

"Hello! I suppose you're Félix?" I started.

"I never saw you around here," he said.

"I just got out of the boat, a few hours ago to be exact."

"But I have seen *you* around," said the lady while managing to look down on Nathaniel in spite of being shorter.

"Hello, madame Reine," said the boy, his tone actually smoothed down and polite.

"I always thought you'd end up in the worst possible place," said Félix. "But the Police? The Pirate Cove Police?"

"See *that's* a better name," said Nathaniel.

"I don't mean to be rude," I interrupted, "but is it all right if I start with the investigation?"

"Investigation?" asked Reine. "About Lady Winchester? It's not like her first disappearance ever!"

She and her husband shared a smile, as loaded as a Christmas dinner in a fisherman's pub.

"I'm sure you have a lot to say about the Admiral's wife's habits, but now we have two people who reported her missing, one of them fearing for her life."

"Two people," said Félix. "Of course Winchester's one of them, the man knows his duties like a donkey knows the way home. And the other one..."

"It wouldn't happen to be Solomon, would it?" asked Reine.

"Is it of any relevance to you?"

The couple had another silent exchange, but this time it felt more like a war council.

"It's not only that he's genuinely a bad person," said Félix, "but Solomon Quickbit almost always means very, very bad news."

"Just like you, Nathaniel," added Reine, "but in a dangerous way."

"Thank you, madame Reine," replied Nathaniel.

"What kind of bad news?" I asked.

"The people who share Solomon's company tend to end up as dead as the cabin boy on the Flying Dutchman," said Félix.

"Well in my defense," Nathaniel said, "no one around me has ever met that fate."

"No one?" asked Reine with her eyebrows so high they almost went over her head.

"It's all about perspective, really..." Nathaniel's voice trailed off. "Anyway, this is not about me, we had questions to ask, didn't we mister Gates?"

I have to admit, I was greatly enjoying seeing Nathaniel so uncomfortable. I could see myself spending more time with that couple.

"I guess we do," I admitted after a short hesitation.

I started walking around the little shop, pretending to be interested in the various wares exposed on the shelves. There were bottles of all shapes, round, elongated, squarish, that bore hand-written labels with names such as "Heavy Mercury", "Buckthorn Syrup",

"Nightshade", "Frogs Lungs", "Arsenopyrite"... When I read "Stag's Vigorous Privates", I decided to get to the point.

"You see, Admiral Winchester seems to believe that you gave some, er, potion, if I remember correctly, to his wife."

The first thing I got was a couple of blank, unfriendly stares.

"I thought you weren't here to cause us problems," said Félix with a good dollop of threat in his voice.

"Not at all, not at all, I am just gathering information. For now. So I take it that this statement is true?"

"We are apothecaries, mister... Gates, is it?" said Reine. "We sell medicine to almost everyone on this island."

"And may I ask what kind of medicine Lady Winchester needs?"

"A part of our trade is to respect people's private lives. I'm sure Nathaniel here wouldn't want people to know what kind of ointments he got from us..."

"I-I-I think mister Gates gets the point, don't you, mister Gates? It's that thing they call, erm, a trade secret?"

He was turning all funny kinds of reds.

"It felt as if Admiral Winchester was hinting at a *subversive* kind of medicine," I said. "He may have mentioned something of a more mystical nature."

I may as well have insulted their family to the tenth generation. Their eyes turned almost entirely black.

"You're talking about voodoo," Reine snapped.

"This has Winchester written all over it," Félix added. "He can't see black folk doing medicine, just 'voodoo'. But whether he likes it or not, this is what we do. If you want medical help, advice, serious treatments for health problems, come to us. But if it's superstition and hocus pocus you're looking for..."

"...go see Wilbur, the Witch doctor."

The contempt in their tone was almost palpable.

"Wilbur?"

"Yes, he comes from the gutters of London, although his life story changes every once in a while."

"And you believe Lady Winchester may have gotten... Something from that Wilbur?"

"Sadly, many people do. When problems are less material and more spiritual, as you put it, there's a tendency to turn towards the occult."

"So maybe we should pay him a visit as well," I said looking at Nathaniel.

He nodded, clearly happy to have an excuse to leave.

"Very well," I concluded.

I walked around, trying to recollect my thoughts before wrapping things up with the apothecaries.

"I do have one last question. I know you are bound by the, how did you call it? The secret of your trade. But do you think Lady Winchester had an ailment that could have anything to do with her disappearance?"

The two had one final silent back and forth. Eyebrows curled. Eyelashes shivered. Frowns could be felt, but not seen. It takes years of living together to achieve such a level of communication. This was almost telepathy.

Finally:

"None that we can think of," said Reine.

Félix stared fixedly at a tiny window in a back corner of the shop.

"Well then, thank you for your time. Please do let me know if you remember anything of interest. Our offices are in Marvin's Reach."

"Marvin's Reach," Félix said with a large smile. "They saved the best for you I see."

"And Nathaniel, your ointments are ready," Reine said. "You can pick them up as soon as you can pay."
"Yes, have a good day!" he said while sprinting for the door.
He was out so fast I barely had the time to tip my hat goodbye.

~

"So, an ointment eh?" I asked him outside.
"Trade secret mister Gates!"
"What trade? You're not an apothecary, are you?"
"Neither are you, so it's literally none of your business. Plus, we have much to do."
"Good to see that now, you're all about the job."
He thought of something witty to reply. I could see it in his smile.
But I heard nothing of it.
I felt a sharp pain in the back of my head. Sharp like neatly polished wood. And I saw a very bright light that completely blinded me.
I put the two elements together, and came to the conclusion that my head had been bashed in.
Which is why I made the sensible decision to pass out entirely.

Chapter 3

"What do we do with a drunken sailor?"

That was a good blow to the head.

Bells were still echoing where my brains were supposed to be when I came back to.

Next thing I noticed, we were in some sort of cove, surrounded by high cliffs. Nathaniel was there too. The poor lad was attached to a wooden pillar covered with barnacles. A more thorough inspection revealed that so was I.

Also, we were chest deep in the sea.

It was the perfect place to keep your boat away from prying eyes. Which made it also ideal to dispose of a couple of undesirables.

"Rise and shine!" Nathaniel greeted me.

"Is this a local tradition?"

He made a face.

"Yeah, I guess you could say that."

I looked around, and noticed a third pillar. It was also covered in barnacles, old, and on its way to fading away in the sea.

And just like ours, it had a poor idiot attached to it.

Only that poor idiot had been dead long enough to have all the skin washed off his bones. His empty sockets stared at me, and he was all smiles.

"So what happens now? Do we get some sort of speech about the virtues of minding our own business?"

"No, we don't do speeches around here."

He tried to wiggle himself a bit out of his ropes, and winced.

"Yup. Leave it to a sailor to tie proper knots."

He cleared his throat, and spat towards our bony companion. His aim was off by a few inches to the right.

"And that's all we get to do now. Until the tide comes in, that is."

"Aren't the tides mild in the Caribbean?"

"Well it's all a matter of perspective. They won't cover much land, so strictly geographically speaking, yes, they're pretty mild. One could even say we don't have any."

He spat once again, this time with a head twist meant to add momentum. It landed on the pole, far above the skeleton's skull.

"But if you see it from our point of view, as puny humans, that water level is going to go up a bit less than a foot, which is just enough to sensibly change our situation."

"I see."

The wind rose, causing a series of wavelets to cover our heads. It didn't last more than a few seconds, but it took away the little comfort we had. We both huffed and puffed to get rid of the water trying to enter our airways.

"And if there's a storm, we won't even have to wait for the tide."

"So many blessings to count."

The most obvious solution was to get my head a bit further from the surf. These were strong ropes, but they had been soaking in salt water for a while, which meant they were probably easier to stretch.

I took hold of the pole with my feet, and started pushing up, helped by the barnacles. The rope dug into my arms, but I was able to make some progress.

"You know, these ropes were used to tie a fully grown Galleon to the harbor," Nate said. "To keep it in place during big storms and all."

"That's why my plan is not to break free, but just to wiggle myself a bit higher."

"That would have been a fantastic idea had you been a little more on the lean side."

"I didn't say I was going to slide up to the top, just, you know..."

I gave up explaining, and chose to save all my energy for the pushing.

"Watch out not to cut yourself," he said.

"You mean for sharks? Them being able to smell a drop of blood in tons of water and all?"

"What? No, that's a myth. Tried it many times and it did nothing."

He spat again. And missed.

"What I meant was, there's nothing worse than having an open wound in salt water. Hurts worse than an army of rabid crabs."

I pushed up again, trying to pry my shoulders out. Nathaniel stopped discouraging me, and went back to his game of whack a skull. The score was still to the dead guy's advantage.

At one point, I felt something yield.

I couldn't tell if it was the rope or one of my bones dislocating itself, but there definitely was some shifting. I started swinging left and right with more gusto, and the yielding intensified.

"And this is what this old man can do with these big ship ropes," I gloated.

"You don't seem to-"

A deep cracking sound came out of the water.

"Well done, it looks like you've managed to break that old pole!"

I won't lie, I did feel a smidgeon of pride. However, the good feeling was to be short-lived.

"You can swim, right?" he asked me.

I froze. Englishmen were known for being many things, but great swimmers wasn't one of them.

"All right I'll be quick," he said, "but listen properly. There was this slaver called Jean Barbot who wrote about the people of a place called Mina, on the west coast of Africa."

"I really think you need to get to the point a bit faster," I urged him while my pole slowly began its descent.

"Yes, quite right. Anyway, apparently, these people had a very peculiar way of swimming that properly baffled Jean Barbot and his men."

"Who?"

"Jean Barbot. The slaver, you are not following. As I was saying, these folks swam by paddling with their feet. And as for their arms, that's the brilliant bit, you're going to love it, they moved them like the arms of a windmill."

"A windmill? How can that *possibly* help?"

"You have to do it sideways, not in front. It propels you forward."

That's as far as I got in Nathaniel's swimming lesson.

The wood cracked, right above my feet. The top part (to which I was attached) just plunged backwards, and I followed with a big splash.

"If it's in any way possible," shouted Nathaniel, "try to make yourself very light!"

"Wh...?" I started, but then the log flipped, the laws of physics having decided that my place should be at the keel and not on the deck of this improvised ship. Better yet, I was dragging it down. So much for making myself very light.

All I could think of was Nathaniel laughing at my failed attempt. Instead of escaping, I actually managed to do the exact opposite. But my legs were free.

I opened my eyes to try to establish where the shore was. With a bit of luck, I could paddle my way towards the beach, and turn things around.

Only one problem: I saw nothing. My eyes burned, and all I could make out were wiggly shapes I hoped to be seaweed.

Since I had practically no air in my lungs, taking my time was not an option. I pivoted around towards where I *thought* the shore was, and just paddled forward.

The stakes were high. If I swam into Nathaniel, it was over, especially since the bugger would probably kick me. If I swam in any direction that wasn't the shore, it was over as well. My eyes were adjusting to the cold underwater darkness, but all I managed to do was confirm that there was sand at the bottom of the sea.

My lungs were painfully empty. They started throbbing. Either I got to shore immediately, or I was passing out again. And this time for good.

A ray of sunshine broke through, and I had a clear view of the sea floor. But instead of coming up towards me, it went deeper.

Out of nowhere, dozens of tiny little yellow fish appeared, slithering around me like crazed piranhas.

But these weren't sea creatures.

They were the little spots that appear in one's vision when the brain is about to lock the front door and leave the keys under the mat.

That was it. A stupid way to die, but they say you don't get to choose.

Well I chose to choose.

All I had to do was breathe in deeply. My end, my own terms.

I felt like I hit something. I heard the wooden bump of my log on some hard surface. I *had* reached the shore.

I stretched my legs down to feel the sand, but found nothing. False alert, I was nowhere near being saved.

So I took a deep breath, anticipating the burn of water rushing in my lungs...

And got fresh air instead. The smell of fish was there, but minus the nasty wetness.

"Well that's a first!" said a feminine voice.

Chapter 4

"Put him in bed with the captain's daughter"

I saw a blurry shape surrounded by a fiery red aura bend over me. A hand grabbed my chest. Another pulled out what seemed to be a sword, and struck me with it.

But instead of feeling the bite of steel in my skin, I recognized the sound of a blade cutting through thick rope. Then the arm lifted me up with no sign of effort (I'm on the upper side of two hundred and forty pounds), and threw me on a wooden floor.

I turned on my side, and dry heaved. I could hear Nathaniel screaming things, probably asking for help. But for the moment, his demands were very low on my list of priorities.

Once my breathing and thought process were back to a semblance of normalcy, I took a good look at my savior.

The red aura turned out to be an impressive copper mane that curled in all directions. I went with my instinct and assumed they were a she, with a long brown leather coat, and thick boots.

"You wouldn't happen to be Lady Winchester, would you?" I asked.

One of her eyebrows shot up, and she hit me in the face, thankfully with the hand that didn't hold the sword.

"I was called a lot of things, but never that! Is this how you thank people for saving you?"

"Apologies," I answered while massaging my bruised jaw, "we were in the middle of an investigation involving that lady, and so..."

"And so you thought 'oh, here's a lady, maybe it's her'!" she scoffed.

"Hey, *I* didn't get your name wrong," shouted Nathaniel. "Can you throw him overboard and save *me* instead?"

She seemed to give it some thought, but I was done flirting with death for the day.

I pulled myself up on one knee, and tried to look as charming as possible.

"I'm Charles Gates, the newly appointed constable of the city. I am in your debt, as well as deeply sorry for having wrongly assumed your identity."

"You know what they say about assuming!" Nathaniel brayed.

"So you're the new *Gendarme*!" she interrupted, and laughed.

I swallowed the little pride I had left, and waited.

"Well mister Gates, welcome aboard my ship," she continued, not entirely done with the laughing. "I am Captain Clarisse Redmayne, former pirate, and master of New Cayenne's one and only shipyard."

"See, I knew that!" said Nathaniel.

"You may rise, mister Gates," she told me.

I stood up with the grace of an old smoker with arthritis.

"I see where the name Redmayne comes from."

"It's actually my real name, not a Blackbeard gimmick."

"You know Captain Teach doesn't like to be called that!" Nathaniel felt the need to add.

"You know very well that's a load of seagull dung!" she shut him up. Then to me: "why is he with you?"

"Nathaniel here is my assistant."

"Nate? Little Sticky Fingers Nate? With the long arm of the law?"

"It's not like I had a choice, or-" he began, but the rest of his sentence was drowned under a vicious little wave.

"He's still on probation," I said. "I would be grateful to have him on board as well."

Redmayne rolled her eyes. With a stroke of her oar, she got us closer to my young associate.

"You still remember how to swim?" she asked him.

Before he could reply, she slashed his ropes with her cutlass, causing Nathaniel to slip under water.

"I hope his answer was going to be yes," I said.

"So, Mister Gates, you were saying you were hot on the trail of Kathy Winchester?"

"I did not know her first name, but yes, we are looking into her disappearance."

"Right."

Nathaniel burst out of the surf, spraying water like an overly excited whale, and made for the ship.

"I suppose you don't know much about the Winchesters and their... Place on the island?" she asked me.

"I get the impression that they are at odds with almost everybody."

Nathaniel climbed in the boat, and sprawled himself on the floor like a mop.

"This little guy here knows about them. Don't you Nate?" she said, poking him with the tip of her boot.

He turned a doleful eye towards her.

"They're rich and annoying," he answered.

"Or maybe are you just jealous that they're successful pirates? And that they're not indebted to everyone and their dog?"

"Hey, I'm paying my debts, as you can very well see."

"By getting my deck all wet?"

She sat at the front bench, and started rowing away from the cove.

"So would you have an idea of who wants us dead?" I asked her.

"Why would I? I build ships, that's what I do. Besides, this town is run by pirates. Knowing their relationship with everything that has to do with authority and the like, I'm tempted to say that nearly everyone here wants you dead."

"Yes, I understand I'll have to wait a bit before I win any popularity contest."

"And that doesn't discourage you?"

I scratched the corner of my eye.

"Jack Boots wants me here."

"Mayor Boots? Isn't he retiring?"

"Yes, which reminds me, I should pay him a visit before he leaves. Maybe he has some tips for me."

"I think it would be 'retire early'," said Nathaniel, still lying on the deck floor.

"Before you see anyone," she said, "I suggest you go talk to Winchester. The man is powerful, and you don't want to be on his bad side."

"He's only one man."

"Money makes him more than just one man."

"Fine, I guess I'll do that. But how do I get to him without ending up in that cove again?"

"I'll drop you at the bottom of Lilac Hill. His mansion is near the top. Get in his good graces, and you may add a few years to your life expectancy."

"I understand you don't know me very well, with us having just met and all, but I'm not very fond of begging for favors."

"You prefer drinking incoming tides?"

"I've drunk worse."

Nathaniel chuckled while scratching his belly.

We approached the western side of the town, which lay on a high cliff, covered with imposing trees, lavish mansions, and quite appropriately, blooming lilacs.

"There you go," said Redmayne. "But be quick. Avoid shadowy corners, or even plain corners for that matter. Your escape was probably noticed, and those who did that to you will try a more efficient approach next time."

"Do I have to go as well?" whined Nathaniel.

"You sure as hell aren't staying on my boat!"

"But I don't want to die... Plus, I'm still wet."

Redmayne drew out her cutlass.

"All right, all right! I can tell when I'm not wanted!"

"That's because you get a lot of practice, Nate. Now out!"

We stepped on the rocks at the bottom of Lilac Hill. It would be an interesting race up.

"Godspeed mister Gates."

"I'll try."

Chapter 5

"Put him in bed with the captain's daughter" part 2

"That's not a good idea," said Nathaniel as we walked up between the sweet smelling trees.

"For some reason, I don't think you qualify as a competent judge of 'good ideas'," I replied.

"Some people want us dead, and right now, we're just jumping back into their open arms."

I halted, contemplating a passage between a large tree and a rock with sharp edges.

"So what would you suggest?" I asked.

"Don't grab that branch, it's obviously half broken. Take the one behind instead."

At a quick glance, his suggestion seemed sensible. So I did as he told me.

"And for our situation?"

"We should go to Mayor Boots. He's the one who wants you here, and he has a bit of authority on this island."

"Yes, I understand that part, but the man is retiring. Heaven knows what kind of man that new guy is, Bartholomew...?"

"Bartholomew James. All the more reason to go there first. Get to know him. Give him a good impression. Make him feel special."

"We'll get to it eventually, I-"

With a loud crack, the branch broke and I fell. I would have gotten all the way to the bottom if it hadn't been for another big tree on which I crashed.

"I guess my branch was the better choice," I said.

"I'm still sticking to my point of view," he insisted.

"The branch was rotten."

"And so is your plan. Don't expect me to stick around when things really go south."

"You mean this isn't south enough?"

~

If we set aside a few treacherous stones and a very resentful badger, the rest of our trip up to the Admiral's mansion was uneventful.

Unfortunately, I don't believe in luck.

Had thugs with sharp knives been hell-bent on taking care of us, we would have heard of them by then. And that would have been reassuring. The world would have made sense, at the very least.

But when things get too easy, my pessimism alarm bells jangle wildly.

"Nice place," I told Nathaniel.

"Too big. Too showy."

"The arcades are pretty, though."

"The man saw Cuba, was awestruck by Spanish royal architecture, and never entirely recovered."

I chuckled.

We walked to the front gate, where two guards eyed us malevolently.

"Hullo!" I said. "Charles Gates, from the New Cayenne Police Squad."

Nathaniel groaned. They kept their gaze on me.

"We're here for an audience with Admiral Winchester, at his request, concerning serious business."

The one I spoke to looked at the other, who was busy giving me the evil eye. He then looked back at his pal, and they both seemed to hesitate.

I know they were wondering if I was bluffing. I sounded too boastful, and they itched to shut me up. But there was a risk that it would cost them greatly if it turned out I was actually important.

After a bout of extensive soul-searching, the first one turned to me. "Very well. Just make sure to inform the servants of your presence."

"Why thank you!"

I walked in as if I had owned the place. I had no idea where all this confidence came from. I was like a hare in a lion's den, minus the ability to run fast. Then again who knows? Maybe hares have the same kind of last-minute bravado right before becoming minced meat.

I looked at Nathaniel, and he frowned back. I wondered how long it would be before he jumped boats.

The man liked to brag. A lot of his personality revolved around talking a big game. But I knew that this wasn't an empty threat. He was a professional deceiver with a quick wit, who could pull the rug from under my feet and disappear before my ass hit the floor.

As I was about to knock on one of the massive double doors, they swung open, revealing an old pirate that was all sneer.

"What is it you want?" he sputtered all over us.

In such a setting, I had expected a classier welcome. Maybe even a wig.

"Erm, hi, I'm Charles Gates, chief of the New Cayenne Law Enforcement. Forces."

Nathaniel snorted.

"Whodat? Oh yes! You're that copper man, yes..."

He did a complete mental inventory of my person with his sneer, the way one tries to find something interesting in a pile of fertilizer.

"The Admiral said you might turn up..."

What was left unsaid but not unheard, was that we were expected in the same way you expect a couple of rats to show up in your food cellar.

"Follow me then."

He turned, and led us through a series of large rooms, a library, a reception room, a dining room, a wide flight of stairs, finally to arrive in a small waiting chamber, with wooden benches.

"There you go," he gestured towards the seats.

He walked to a double leaf door, and knocked three times on it.

"M'lord, it's that Gates man here to see you!"

Then to us.

"He'll call you when he's ready."

Sneer left.

"*That Gates man,*" I mused.

"At least he mentioned you," Nathaniel replied sourly.

"They don't like you around here, do they?"

"Well pirates aren't exactly known to be easy to live with, didn't they teach you that in police school?"

"But in *your* case, it feels like a whole new level of not liking."

"Let's say I ruffled many feathers, and some birds tend to hold a grudge."

"I have yet to meet a bird around here who likes you."

"Oh, so you've met like, what, four people in town, and now it's everyone? Bit of a faulty logic there, isn't it?"

"Sure, but as far as I'm concerned, it's a hundred percent of the people I've met. And it's six people, to be exact. Seven with this one."

"You're just meeting the wrong kind of people."

"Without a doubt."

I stared at the walls, which were heavily decorated with ornamental weapons. The whole display felt clunky and off balance.

"So, what do you plan to do with the big guy?" Nathaniel asked while pointing a thumb towards the office doors. "Bring out your warmest smile, apologize for being so cavalier earlier, tell him you didn't really mean it?"

"You know me so well. And by the way, I never went to police school."

"You don't say. Considering how fast you're moving with this case, I am shocked."

"Sorry if I made you miss teatime. And as for *the big guy*, I'm not too keen on crawling on all fours in front of anyone, powerful or not."

He raised a skeptic eyebrow.

"All right," I admitted, "I may be gentler this time, but that's because you catch more flies with honey than you do with vinegar. One has to keep his feet on the ground."

"There it is."

"It makes no sense to maintain an animosity with someone for absolutely no reason."

"Then why start it in the first place?"

"I just wanted to make sure everyone knew where their place was."

"Oh, I get it, so after this, you'll also rush to Solomon and buy him a drink?"

"I just need to properly understand how things work around here."

"Well it sure seems you understand the golden rule: the powerful people are the ones who matter, and the rest are part of the background. Looks like you'll fit right in after all."

I didn't expect it to sting.

"I'm here to make the best of a crappy situation. Going to Boots would have been the same. Unless you don't think the mayor is powerful."

"He's powerful because the important people want him to be. He's appointed to be powerful. Poor guy, once he's out of office, he'll be back to being a nobody, like the rest of us. But Winchester here..."

"Not so loud!" I tried to whisper.

"Exactly. The man isn't an official or anything, when you think of it. But since he's got loads of shiny metals and stones, even *you* are minding your p's and your q's, not just in his presence, but merely within earshot."

"Yes, all right, I get your point, and I wholeheartedly agree with you. But there's a time and place for everything. And yes, I will go buy Solomon Quickbit a pint once all of this is over. Unless he's guilty."

I stopped to catch my breath, surprised at how personally I was taking this.

"You know what?" I said, "just wait and see how I deal with it, and you'll... You'll just have to see, I guess."

"That you don't suck up to the rich?"

I made an effort not to react.

There was a little clock in the upper corner of the room. In the silence that followed, the ticking sounded quite loud.

"He doesn't seem to mind to keep you waiting, does he?" said Nathaniel. "I mean, that's no way to treat the head of the N.C.R.E.A.F.M.L., is it?"

"The N.R. what?"

"If we're to have a stupid acronym, might as well go big. We can figure out what it means later."

I cleared my throat.

"Waiting is not necessarily a bad thing in itself, and making people wait is not always a lack of respect. Good things happen to those who wait."

Even the ticking of the clock managed to sound sarcastic.

I stood up.

"But there is such a thing as overdoing it, I suppose."

I faced the door, and hated myself for having that fear of the rich and powerful. I knocked too hard, probably in order to compensate. Nothing happened.

"That was loud enough, wasn't it?"

"I'm pretty sure it prompted the mangy old crow to open the main entrance downstairs."

"So what, he's ignoring us?"

I knocked again.

"Admiral Winchester, I'm afraid that time is not on our side," I said through the door.

Tic toc, tic toc.

"Maybe he fell asleep?" Nate suggested.

I grabbed the handle, summoning all the working class rage I could muster, and turned.

I had half-hoped for it to be locked, but it wasn't.

Slowly, I pushed the door, and inserted my face in the opening.

"Admiral...?"

Something was wrong. He was sitting behind his desk, hands on the armrests, his eyes on me. It wasn't a welcoming stare, but it wasn't filled with rage either. He looked... Oddly neutral.

"Admiral Winchester?"

I stepped in, and walked up to his desk.

"I apologize for barging in, but it so happens that-"

That's when I put two and two together.

In the waiting room, I had noticed that the decorations were not well balanced. I finally understood it was because one of the swords was missing.

How did I reach such a bold conclusion?

Because that sword was busy sticking out of Winchester's chest. It also explained the dark brown spot on his shirt I had mistaken for an unusual fashion choice.

"I have to admit," said Nathaniel who had snuck up behind me, "I had not expected you to do *that*."

Chapter 6

"The sharks got his body and the devil got his soul (oh poor old man)"

I couldn't get my eyes off the dead body.

"You really did stick it up to him, I have to give you that. Or more like, stick it up *in* him."

"Oh stop it, you know very well I have nothing to do with it."

"Considering I'd be entitled to have doubts, me not knowing you well and all that, I'm afraid the, erm, what do you call that thing? The evidence! Yes, I'm afraid the evidence is arguably against you."

He was right. As far as everyone was concerned, Winchester was alive and well when we arrived.

"Told you we should have gone to Mayor Boots first."

"Can we focus on the subject at hand? The sensible thing should be to call for help, right?"

"Ah yes, the oldest trick in the book. Kill the man, and then act as if you're here to help." He waved a finger at me. "Pirates don't fall for that one."

"But it's not…" I began, then realized he was right. We were too far into that trap to just step out of it.

That's why it had been so easy to make it there. A mob resolute on avenging Winchester's death would be less merciful with us than the tide had been. When men like him get killed, death sentences are quick to be given, and even quicker to be carried out. Regardless of the fairness of the trial, it goes without saying.
"So what do we do?" I asked.
Nathaniel walked towards one of the windows, and examined the backyard.
"Lots of guards, we can't exactly hop down in the garden."
"But that would make things worse! Escaping would be a confirmation of our guilt."
"You're still thinking like a regular. When in pirate land, do as pirates do."
"So what, you expect us to prance away from this predicament by swinging our swords, throwing out a few witty insults, grabbing on to chandeliers, yo-ho-ho and a bottle of rum?"
"I didn't say we should live one of your landlubber's fantasies. Just..."
He scrutinized the room, the cupboards, the ceiling, even the library. He dwelled on it longer than I cared for.
"This can't be!" he exclaimed.
"This can't be what?"
He walked towards a particular shelf, and zeroed in on a book.
"He has it! Unbelievable!"
"What? What in the world are you talking about?"
"This!" He took it out. "Blackbeard's Cookbook!"
I did not have the reaction he expected. I didn't have *any* reaction, for that matter.
"Don't you know how huge this is?"
"You haven't by any chance forgotten about our little problem?"

"Chas, this is Blackbeard's Cookbook! It's the Holy Grail of pirates! Even bigger!"

"It's a cookbook. And don't call me Chas."

"Blackbeard's Cookbook!" Nathaniel insisted.

"What, does it have a treasure map or something?"

"Have you lived all your life under a rock?"

"You're the one living under a rock! Where I come from, problems aren't solved by marveling at books on food!"

He looked at me the way a teacher looks at the kid who drew a stick figure on the math assignment.

"Or," he replied, "we could go back to the waiting room, close the door, and reassume our initial positions. Had you not been so impatient, we wouldn't be in such a mess."

"Sweet heavens you have *got* to be the worst assistant in the world!"

"So we're not doing that either?"

I let out an irritated sigh.

"Yes, I guess it's the least idiotic thing to do..."

We walked back out quietly, making sure no one had arrived in the waiting room, and delicately closed the door. The *click* made us wince.

Nathaniel sat down, crossed his legs, and slouched.

I imitated him, not happy at all with myself for playing this game.

He gave me a disapproving glance.

"What?" I snapped.

"You're not credible."

"What do you mean I'm not credible?"

"It doesn't look like you've been sitting here all this time."

"That's because I wasn't."

"Well it doesn't help you look innocent, even though you think you are."

"But I *am* innocent! I can't believe I have to go through all this effort just to prove the obvious."

"Do you usually sit like this?"

I looked down.

"What's wrong with my sitting?"

"You look like a classless slob."

"Thank you, I was following your lead."

"Yes, you are rubber and I am glue, but the thing is, you have to sit in a way that *is* you. I sit like a spoiled aristocrat because I like people to look at me this way."

I snorted loudly, but he carried on without flinching.

"You have to make people *believe* in the way you're sitting. You like to pretend you're strong-willed and domineering."

"It's not pretend."

"Sure, but nobody cares. Just sit in a similar way, give me that image."

I glared at him.

"Go on. They will be here any minute now."

With all the resentment in the world, I shifted positions.

"Not bad, there's a glimmer of authenticity. I'm sure you can do better."

"Much appreciated. Anything else?"

"Now that you mention it, I may have some interesting suggestions as to what to call our little... Organisation."

I refrained from groaning.

"By all means."

"You see, you're always going on with law enforcement this, and police that, but you're missing out on something crucial."

"And that is?"

"We're a police for pirates, Chas."

"Don't call me Chas, and I don't like where this is going."

"Give it a chance, Chas."

"I'm not in a giving mood."

"The New Cayenne Pirate Police!"

It wasn't actually so bad, but I wasn't ready to give in so easily.

"The N.C.P.P.?"

"I know, right? Sounds hard. Sounds like we mean business."

"Sounds like an excuse to spray spittle on people."

"Exactly, it's perfect! I first thought of Law and Plunder, but it felt a bit corny."

"I hate them both equally."

"Sleep on it, and come back to me. I swear, it'll grow on you."

"I *do* like the idea of making it alive to bedtime, though."

The door to the staircase opened, and I flinched.

"You boys are still here?" asked Sneer.

"It appears so," I said.

"Well that's odd. The Admiral likes to make people wait, but never so long. Unless he really hates you."

"I guess you have your answer then."

Nathaniel gave me a look that meant I was overdoing it. Or that he discovered he had hemorrhoids.

Sneer went to the door, but this time, he knocked hard enough to make the hinges jangle.

"M'lord? Is everything all right?"

He looked at us, and we replied with big round interrogation marks in our eyes.

"I'm coming in, M'lord."

He opened as quickly as respect allowed him to, and stepped in.

"What's this?" he shouted. Then much, much louder: "Alarm! Raise the alarm! The Admiral has been slain!"

He had the voice of a man who could make himself heard from bow to stern during a thundering storm. Which is why within seconds, the office and the waiting room were filled with guards and servants.

We stood up, doing our best "what in heaven's name is going on?" impression.

"*Grab these two men*," yelled Sneer, pointing at us.

"I demand you tell us immediately what is happening!" I barked with as much authority as I could muster, "and if anyone so much as lays a finger on us, two officers of the law, we shall have you all arrested!"

"I knew you two were up to no good," continued Sneer, "Admiral Winchester did warn me. But to come and stab the man in his very home, that's just despicable!"

"How dare you accuse us of such a thing! We are..."

I stopped talking. Even if I had said we were Saint Hornigold come to give them chests full of diamonds, they seemed determined to squash us like a couple of cockroaches scurrying on the kitchen floor.

"You two are to be tried and hung for the murder of his lordship the Admiral of Winchester!" recited Sneer.

"If it's worth anything, we're the ones supposed to make sure fair trials happen," I tried.

It did not cause much of a stir.

"And it's 'hanged', not 'hung'. We're people, not paintings."

We were promptly chained to each other, and led down the stairs. Things could have looked better.

Chapter 7

"So early in the morning, a pirate likes his bottle-o"

The Admiral had an impressive cellar, filled with enough weapons and alcohol to withhold at least a three-month siege.

They chained us to wine barrels in the beverages part of the premises, because no one brings a bottle of rum to a musket fight.

"Try anything funny, and your sentence will be carried out faster than you can reach back to scratch your arses!" Sneer said before leaving us.

I looked at Nathaniel.

"So we're dead by the end of the day?"

"It all depends on how fast they manage to assemble our jury."

"There's an actual jury?"

"Yes, we're pirates, not a London mob."

"Oh right, the famous 'pirate code'."

"You, my friend, have got to get rid of all of Nan's bedtime stories about life. There is no 'code'."

"Didn't captain Roberts write one down?"

"Probably, but he doesn't speak for all of us. We do, however, have a set of rules. We elect our captains. We give proper burials to our dead, when the body isn't at the bottom of the sea. And we have judges and trials for criminals like us."

"So when there's a misunderstanding such as this, we actually have a chance?"

He grimaced.

"It's not like we're a perfect society either. There's a reason why you were hired."

"How wonderfully ironic, isn't it?"

"It was bound to happen, at least the first few tries. But at least, it will allow our successors to learn from our mistakes."

"You sure have a knack for finding the silver lining."

"I'm a born optimist, what can I say?"

I tried to budge my barrel, wanting to see if I could tip it over, but it turned out to be as heavy as it looked.

"Judging by your luck so far," said Nathaniel, "the only way you'll get your cask to move is to have it crush you."

"Probably. Although I'm not sure it wouldn't be better than hanging from an itchy rope until I choke to death."

"It's all a matter of taste."

I gave a sharp pull forward, which led to my head banging back on the wood. It hurt a bit, but it also sparked an idea.

I let myself slide down as low as I could, and lifted my leg up high. The tip of my boot made contact with the barrel.

"Impressive. You're still very flexible for a seventy year-old man."

"I'll take that as a compliment coming from a prepubescent lad. And don't lose faith; maybe next year, you'll get to shave like the big boys."

I punctuated that last comment by kicking harder.

"If I was into weathered, corpulent men, I'd be looking at you in a very different light right now," he said.

The kick hadn't made a dent, but I felt as if the wood could give in a little. My back painfully voiced its disapproval, but I kicked again. A plank shifted.

"Joke aside, are you really thinking of breaking this oak barrel? This heavy, bulky, made to travel from the English Channel to the stormy West Indies barrel, by just kicking it with the strength of a baby stretching his legs?"

I answered with a stronger blow. I was about to say how I pictured myself kicking him in the nether regions for motivation, but the wood yielded, and my foot broke through.

For a second, I was trapped in a highly undignified position.

"Well done!" shouted Nathaniel. "We are saved now!"

I pulled my foot free, and was immediately doused in about five bottles' worth of red wine. I may or may not have ingested part of it.

"You know, you might be on to something. Let's turn this into a party, and we won't even feel the execution part of the trial."

I was trying to spit out what I hadn't swallowed. As I jerked around, I felt the other planks breaking loose.

I paused for a second, embracing the idea of being literally drowned in wine. The breach was still releasing gusts that made their way to my not entirely closed mouth.

"You could at least share," said Nathaniel.

"Just do as I do," I managed.

"I'm sorry, but I actually have a sense of decorum, unlike others."

"Suit yourself."

Channeling my best impression of the enslaved man breaking himself free from his chains, I thrusted my shoulders forward.

In all honesty, I did overdo it a bit. In my defense, I had expected the task to be more challenging.

As it turns out, my barrel was on the very edge of succumbing. It had barely needed a nudge. Which is why the major shove I gave almost shattered it at once.

For a second (or fifteen), I was immersed in an alcoholic's wet dream.

I found myself baptised in wine like an old-school Christian, head and all, very much ready to establish immediate contact with the divine.

"Holy cannonballs!" shouted Nathaniel. "When I asked you to share, I never thought you'd comply with such generosity!"

It was not only what I swallowed, the fumes also crawled up my nostrils to tickle my brain, making everything confusing.

"I'm not going down without getting the second round!" said Nathaniel while swinging his left leg up high.

His first attempt was more successful than mine. The admiral must have used some low-quality wood, the stingy bastard, and the cask just shattered.

"I don't think I ever had so much wine in my life," I said. "At once, I mean."

"Wine? You think this is wine?"

The expression I gave him mustn't have looked too bright.

"This, my good man, is pure, unadulterated, straight out of the sugar cane, rum!"

It seems now relevant to point out that the room we were in was approximately one foot lower than the neighboring ones, and didn't exceed an area of ten foot square.

In other words, it was easy to flood.

When the cask shattered, I wasn't exactly set free. I still had chains on, that went around a bunch of heavy wooden planks. I was pulled backwards and downwards. The rum level would not drown me, but being an inch away from my mouth, it was close enough to do its job.

"Hurry and stand up, before the fumes make you drunk," said Nathaniel.

"Yes, it's not like I'm halfway there."

As I struggled to slide the chains away from the planks, I ended up having a lot more sugar cane juice splashed on my face than I bargained for.

"This is not going to work," he said.

Nathaniel carried on with my barrel-kicking technique, his head underneath the rum level. After only a few blows, the wood shattered, and the wave came in.

We weren't about to drown. By sitting up, we could breathe, while macerating in dark Jamaican rum.

Nathaniel did a better job of getting rid of the planks, and with the chains still hanging from his wrists, he stood up.

"Come on Chas, can't help you if you don't help me."

He reached down, and grabbed my arm.

"Don't call me Chas."

I grabbed him back, and since I was easily twice as heavy, he came tumbling face down, chains and all.

He made a few gurgling sounds, and pulled his face out of the rum.

He crawled behind me, and managed to set me free.

"Come on, you can stand up, now!"

He was right. I was up faster than I had expected to.

"Excellent," I said. "Now, for a good old-fashioned escape..."

My sense of balance was absent from duty for a second, but I retrieved it with the grace of an old scarecrow.

"I can't already be drunk!"

"I know you're British, but that was quite a lot of booze," slurred Nathaniel. "We have to get out before we collapse."

We struggled out of the room that was thankfully doorless.

"Look," he pointed, "there's that trap from where they carry in the wood."

A few steps led up to a small opening meant for logs.

"I hate to break it to you," I articulated, "but I fear that, compared to a tree, I may be a bit too plump."

"You can say that again," he burst out laughing.

I tried not to join him, failed, and it turned into an uncontrollable laughing fit. When all the air was gone from our lungs, it sounded like a lethal hiccup bound to knock us out.

"Oh no," he managed, catching his breath, "so this is how I'm going to die..."

We were beyond redemption.

I did manage to walk up to the opening. I squeezed my head in, then my shoulders.

"See? Can't get very far in there," I turned around and told him, finally getting some self-control.

Catching his breath, still sniggering, he walked towards me, and unceremoniously pushed my arse, a hand on each cheek.

"Ouch!"

"Not so loud," he shushed me with his finger on his nose, "there's guards, guards everywhere!"

"Oh my! Guards everywhere!"

The giggles came back with a vengeance. There was no way we were escaping this.

He did however manage to shove me through the narrow passage, and out in the open.

I stood up and breathed the alcohol-free air.

"It sure smells clean on your island."

"Depends on where you sniff."

He stood up like a newborn fawn.

"Wow, I think I had more than my usual share of rum today," he added.

"The way I see it, all we have to do is make it to the palisade back there, and we'll be free," I said, trying hard to sound actually serious.

Nathaniel looked at it with a highly dubious look on his face.

"You plan to fly? It's, it's very high, and very, very smooth. I mean, spiders, and ants, and... Other crawly creatures with sticky legs, even *they* must have a hard time climbing on that."

"Not if we use the magic of teamwork," I replied with the slyness of the hopelessly drunk.

"I'm not to be used as a... As a ladder, I'll let you know."

"No such thing needed. All you have to do is step on my hands, like this, then you can grab the top of the wall, and pull yourself up. Then, you lend me a hand, and pull *me* up. Wow, my thoughts don't come easy, do they?"

"Do they ever?"

"I will not dignify this with an answer."

"Well done Chas, that's the way to stick up to your bullies."

"I eat bullies like you for breakfast."

"Yuck."

"Yes, I heard it, it sounded better in my..."

A fleeting glimpse into lucidity had me realize we were wasting precious time. I immediately started running towards the stone fence.

"Hey, you could at least finish your..." Nathaniel started.

He then must have realized the same thing, and followed me in an approximately straight line (not that I had any right to judge).

I positioned myself next to the wall, and joined my hands to give him a leg up.

"Up you go!"

His eyes briefly suggested that he was having some sensible ideas against my plan, but the rum swept his doubts away.

"Up I go."

For a reason only known to Henry Morgan, I thought it a jolly good idea to give him an enthusiastic boost the second he stepped on my palms. In spite of my stature, I could tell he needed a bit more height to reach the ledge.

But instead of lifting him gently, I sent him flying face first into the wall.

"Oops!"

Nathaniel screamed long and loud, but one of his hands had gotten a grip on the ledge.

"Hey, you're almost there!" I shouted.

"I swear to you, Charles, I'm getting out of here alone!"

"And you called me Charles! Maybe I should hit you with walls more frequently."

"Give me a push or else I won't make it!"

"And you'll abandon me?"

"Look at it this way. If you help me, there's a fifty percent chance you may escape. If you don't..."

"All right, all right, you don't have to go all statistical on me..."

I grabbed his feet, and placed them on my shoulders.

"Ready?"

"I am. Are you?"

"Just stand up straight!"

A dull pain exploded in my upper back. I knew it would turn into a sharp one once I sobered up.

"Hey, I can totally climb out of here."

"By all means."

"I might even want to save you as well!"

"Do you plan on-"

"Both of you!" shouted a voice behind us. "Stop right there, and turn around very slowly!"

I grunted.

"Can I step down to do this?" asked Nathaniel.

"I said turn around!" insisted the voice.

"That should be fun," I said. "Hang in there, Nate."

I slowly rotated to the right, holding on to my assistant's feet.

I did a pretty decent job maintaining our position, with his chain dangling in front of my face.

And this is how we ended up facing a fairly large group of armed people. There was of course Sneer, plenty of guards, and two official-looking men: a short stout one, and a tall bony one.

"Is that...?" started the short one. "Nathaniel? I ask you to assist our new constable to pay for your crimes, and you immediately go back to committing more crimes?"

"Actually," I said, "I would be the constable."

He glared at me.

"You're Charles Gates?"

I curtsied, which nearly caused Nathaniel to topple over.

"Mayor Boots?" I presumed.

"Why didn't you come to see me as soon as you arrived?" he lectured me.

"Told you so," dropped Nathaniel from above.

Chapter 8

"Put him in the brig until he's sober"

Town Hall was a failed attempt at fanciness that stood in the center of the docks like a monument erected in the name of trying too hard. At least, it had vast windows, from which one could see the ships as well as the gallows.

Mayor Boots sat behind his desk, while the tall, thin one, who must have been his replacement Bartholomew James, stood to his left, a hand on the chair.

Nathaniel and I were facing them, surrounded by the angry mob that had considerably grown on our way there.

"I pronounce these two men guilty of the murder of his lordship the Admiral Winchester!" declared Sneer.

"Now, now, Mister Christopher, this is no longer how we do things around here," replied Boots.

"Making sure justice is served?" asked Mister Christopher, formerly known as Sneer. I liked my nickname better.

"No, declaring people guilty and hanging them willy-nilly, only to realize we got the wrong one, and start all over again until the island's population dies down!"

"But we caught'em red-handed, we did!"

"You found mister Gates with the sword in his hand as it plunged into admiral Winchester's chest?" asked Bartholomew James, with a deep voice that evoked a man who didn't need to shout his orders for them to be promptly executed. Boots didn't seem to mind him taking over.

"Well, er, not exactly *that* red-handed, but, you know..." Sneer's voice faltered. "What I'm saying is, when I had left the admiral, he was alive and well. And after I introduced these two into his waiting room, he was dead."

Disapproving mumbles rustled throughout the audience.

"Plus, it was with a sword stolen from the waiting room. It's clear that these two waited for me to leave, grabbed it, went in uninvited, and stabbed the poor undeserving man!"

He ended his sentence with a hint of forced emotion in his voice. He wasn't just testifying: he was playing the role of his life.

"Thank you, Mister Christopher, but you should leave the deductions to the professionals," said Bartholomew, looking at me.

"It *is* true that the professionals in question seem to be under quite unusual circumstances..."

"They're drunker than two boiled owls on a drifting ship!" said someone in the audience, which caused a wave of laughter. I looked at Nathaniel, and nodded.

"I must admit that the image fits," I said, "but in our defense, it was purely accidental."

The spectators emitted grunts and some half-baked statements meant to express their disbelief.

"Dear mister Gates," said Bartholomew, putting a quick stop to the growing discontent, "as an appointed official, you do not have to justify yourself. You are in the middle of an investigation, an *official* investigation, and cannot, in any possible way, be considered as a suspect."

They all looked dumbfounded.

"He's *looking* for the murderer, he cannot *be* the murderer," he translated.

"But I saw them..." started Sneer.

"You saw them *what*, Mister Christopher?"

"They tried to escape!"

"From being slaughtered by an angry mob! And this is what my predecessor and I are trying to change around here! Good heavens, people, use some common sense! What interest would a perfect stranger being catapulted in the middle of nowhere have in killing a man such as the Admiral?"

"He could be an agent!" said one of Winchester's personal guards. "Sent by Wood Rogers to destroy our community!"

"*Woodes* Rogers' intentions are well known," Bartholomew corrected, "but mister Gates came at Mayor Boots' request, and I intend to fully support him when I take over. He represents the law, and you shall all treat him as such."

"Rogers is the guy who..." Nathaniel started whispering to me.

"Waged war against piracy, I know," I whispered back.

Our drunken whispering drew the attention back to us.

"Sorry," I muttered.

"Mister Christopher," continued Bartholomew, "you are therefore required to immediately undo these shackles, lest you be declared an outlaw."

Sneer stared in disbelief at first, but then got his facial expression back.

"We are a free people here," he slowly hissed.

"True, but if we intend to remain that way," Boots exploded, "we desperately need to follow some kind of order! So, give these men their freedom back, say you're sorry, and just bugger off!"

Sneer took out his keys with as much enthusiasm as if he were getting rid of something sticky on the sole of his shoe. The look he gave me left not much room for interpretation as to the feelings he harbored.

"Sorry, sorry, I'm late," burst in Selena Montgomery, slamming open both doors in a gust of papers. "But I got the summons at the very last minute, and you know how hard it is for me to reschedule everything at the drop of a pin, don't you mayor Boots?"

"Yes, sir, we do apologize, but it was a matter of life and death."

"You mean life *or* death?"

"Both, Mrs Montgomery," said Bartholomew.

She twitched at the use of her name instead of "sir". However, she did not correct him, as I thought she would, but bent down to pick up her papers.

"*His* life," the mayor-to-be pointed at me, "and Admiral Winchester's death."

Nathaniel took an exaggerated look of pained shock for not being acknowledged.

"Winchester's dead?" She dropped a few more pages.

"Admiral Winchester," corrected Sneer, "he worked hard, he did, to get his title, s'not to be brought back to the level of a low-commoner."

"My God, mister Gates," she said, ignoring Sneer, "why are you in shackles and... Hold on, is this rum I smell?"

"Yes sir," said Sneer, "they got drunk and killed my master."

"Hey, get your story straight," said Nathaniel, "you said we got drunk *after* we killed him."

"Holy Moses, we didn't kill anyone!" I jumped in to stop Montgomery from going down some dark lanes in assumption land.

"That's enough, everybody out!" Boots shouted. "Out! And, erm, Mister Christopher?"

"Yes, Mister Mayor?"

"*The shackles*!"

He unchained us, and left with a salute that might as well have been an obscene gesture.

"Good grief!" said the mayor, relieved to be rid of everyone.

"Hold that thought, Jack," said Bartholomew as he tiptoed towards the doors. He delicately grabbed the handles, and swung them open, to reveal at least five former members of the mob, huddled, their heads tilted sideways, an ear towards where the doors used to be.

"Eavesdropping on the affairs of the mayor's office will now be considered as spying, and will promptly be punished as such," he stated gravely.

They scattered.

"Now *that*'s how you talk to pirates," Nathaniel nudged me. "Not so much the words, but the way you say them..."

"All right gentlemen," continued Boots, "and, sir, please sit down." We obediently each took a chair, while Selena Montgomery sat next to the mayors, glad to be finally able to tidy up her papers. Everything in its rightful place.

"How I really, really wish you had come to me first," the mayor began.

"Well, that had been my suggestion," Nathaniel said, "but since you put *him* in charge..."

"Oh, give it a rest," I said, "you were wrong about the branch."

"Right, because that's the same thing..."

"First of all," Boots interrupted us, "you two aren't exactly out of hot water. What Bartholomew did here was buy you some time, but nowhere does it say that the person doing the investigation cannot be the murderer. Especially if you were there *at the time of the bloody murder*!"

Alcohol brings you back to your childhood. It's not that kids act like drunk people, but the other way around. Drunk people act like toddlers. One drink too many, and out comes the little brat, the good, the bad, and the dirty.

Which is why I felt as ashamed as if I had soiled my diaper.

"It was a simple case, wasn't it? Winchester's wife had disappeared, probably a story of scorned love. All you had to do was come to me for some guidance, and it would have probably been solved by teatime. Especially judging by Lady Winchester's antics. Easy as pie."

A headache was starting to creep up from the base of my skull to that little spot between the eyebrows. Time to pay for my drink.

"But now that you decided to go rogue, you've angered the gods of bad luck. It shouldn't surprise you that many around the island don't look favorably on having any sort of law enforcement. I would have told you to remain careful, especially for this first case. It would have helped you settle in and make a strong argument in your favor. You would have been seen as a decent policeman, and New Cayenne would finally have had its established police force. But now..."

Solona jotted down notes, while Bartholomew remained expressionless.

Nathaniel stared at a point near the ceiling.

"Hold on a second," I said. "The way you're putting it, it's almost as if *you* had built that case from scratch, Mister Mayor."

"Well done, you! (Editor's note: before Sherlock Holmes, snarky comments about obvious deductions lacked a certain sass). I'm glad to see your ex-employers hadn't lied about your wit! All you need now is a little common sense, and you should be good to go!"

I tried to make my face as blank and cold as possible.

"So, where's Lady Winchester then?"

"Not a clue!"

"But I thought..."

"The case wasn't built from scratch," said Bartholomew. "Not entirely, at least. Lady Winchester *did* disappear, we just happened to know where she was at the time. But while you two were going on a fool's errand, she managed to slip between our fingers."

"Why then does she keep disappearing?"

"Ha!" laughed Boots, "I'm sorry, but we don't have the time to go over all of Lady Winchester's adventures. She is a highly eccentric woman, and every once in a while, she manages to get herself into some different new problem. Secret societies, the occult, New Piracy, lone ship sailing, flying..."

"Flying?"

"Yes, once, she found in an obscure book the design of some sort of flying machine, and she disappeared for weeks with a band of poor gullible saps willing to help her."

"Did the machine fly?"

"No, but it managed to decapitate her crew."

Nathaniel winced.

"Aye, I remember that one."

"So her escapades do not involve anything of a... Romantic nature?"

"All of them!" said Boots. "You could write a full library of romantic books on her disappearances. Worthy of a good story to tell."

"And this time," I said, "would it happen to be with that Solomon Quickbit?"

The atmosphere in the room grew colder and darker.

"Is that what Quickbit said?" asked Boots.

"Yes, but even Winchester thought he had bedazzled her with some sort of voodoo."

Boots shot a look at Selena. She replied with a frown.

"I'm guessing that this time," I said, "Lady Winchester may have bitten more than she could chew? Is that why Winchester seemed so worried?"

"Quickbit is actually a dangerous man."

"I thought it came with being a pirate?"

This got me a round of dirty looks. Even Bartholomew let go of his enigmatic style to scowl at me.

"There's a difference, a huge gap, a chasm, between honest to God piracy, and downright..." Boots struggled with his words.

"Quickbit's a plague-carrying rat," said Selena.

"He's a serial mutineer," Nathaniel told me from the corner of his mouth.

"Aren't all pirates...?" my question died as I was asking it, thanks to Nate's warning look.

"Mister Gates," said Bartholomew, who had gone back to his composed tone, "Quickbit is known to have killed several pirate captains he was working for *as a pirate*."

"I got it, mutiny with the regulars is acceptable, but is frowned upon within... The industry."

"Well among regulars, it's the only way to change captains," said Nathaniel.

"True, I had forgotten you folks function in a democratic fashion," I apologized. "And Quickbit has violated that."

"Indeed."

"What bothers me," I thought out loud, "is that I don't see why he would have waited until now to kill him, since it automatically makes him a primary suspect. Unless of course, it was to frame us..."

I did not get the reactions I had hoped for. No "we know you didn't do it", no "you're innocent", not even a "we're with you on this". Nothing to make me feel better. Instead, everybody stared at a distant point ahead of them, or underneath the floor.

Boots was peering through his desk, with the look of a man in search of desperate solutions. I had the feeling he was toying with the idea of declaring us guilty, in order to get a fresh start with a new chief of police. I had become, after all, tainted goods.

"So, where was Lady Winchester before she disappeared? You know, when you knew where she was?" I veered the conversation back on its former and less dangerous tracks.

Bartholomew looked at me as if snapping out of a dream. Probably a dream where I was judged for a crime I hadn't committed.

"She was in Drake's End, the shipwreck," he said.

"An actual ship that belonged to Drake?"

"It's the local legend."

"We called it that way to attract tourists," said Boots. "It even worked, for a while. People would be searching all around it for Drake's infamous lost riches. But now, it's just an abandoned old wreck."

"Only Kathy Winchester still finds it irresistibly romantic," said Selena, rolling her eyes.

"Well then, there's no point in wasting time, is there?" I said, standing up. "Come on, Nate, off to the old shipwreck, shall we? This investigation won't progress on its own."

A bit stunned by my sudden burst of energy, Nathaniel stood up, and followed me to the door.

"Thank you gentlemen. Selena, always a pleasure."

I went down the stairs and out in the streets as quickly as I could.

"What just happened?" asked Nathaniel.

"Didn't you see?"

I stopped and turned to face him.

"Didn't you hear them think?"

"They're suspecting us?"

"No, but they're starting to wonder if it wouldn't be more cost-efficient to go along with that storyline."

"You heard them think that?"

"These people do politics. All that matters to them is looks and reputation, and right now, we're becoming more and more a liability. In their place, I would have done the same."

I hastened my pace.

"Why are you in such a hurry?"

"I want to disappear before one of them changes their mind and calls us back. Our immunity is bound to expire, let's not waste a second."

I looked back at the harbor where an execution was taking place.

"Plus we're way too close to the gallows."

Chapter 9

"I'll tell you a tale of the fish and the sea"

The wreck was a frigate that must have looked majestic before it got mercilessly smashed on one of the treacherous rocks that were scattered around New Cayenne. But even from the shore, it looked impressive and ominous.

"When Boots said *old*," I told Nathaniel, "I thought he meant only a few years old. But this… Didn't Columbus arrive in one of these?"

"Maybe not that old, but you sure as hell can't use the wood to build a half-decent raft."

"I mean, it looks one good storm away from being completely washed clean off those rocks."

"Old ships are always sturdier than you'd expect."

He spat on the floor.

"Anyway," he added, "shouldn't we be looking for old Backstab Solomon? The way I see it, if we find him, we save our skins."

"And where were you planning on finding him? Sitting nicely at home, playing with his toes?"

"Not that I want to teach you your own job, but actually spending time looking for him sounds like a good investment, no?"

"Your untrustworthy man sounds like he's used to disappearing without a trace. We have more chances of quickly finding the attention seeker. And when we find her, we are this much closer to finding him."

"Yes, life sure is wonderful in the land of logic."

The wreck could be reached either by boat or by jumping from rock to rock. The first way was the least risky, and the second was the only one we had at our disposal.

"How do you expect tourists to go visit the ship if there's no 'ye olde boat rental shoppe' on the shore?"

"There used to be, but I think we got rid of the boats. Makes the experience more authentic. Do things the hard way, like a true treasure hunting pirate. Arr."

"Or die trying," I said, adjusting my balance on the first rock.

It didn't turn out to be as bad as expected. It did require balance and last-minute decisions, but it was nothing a ten year-old with a death wish wouldn't have been able to manage.

And then I fell in the water.

I swear I was paying attention, and my steps were as steady as a mountain goat's, but for some reason (old age), I slipped, and got myself soaked for the third time that day.

"Rookie mistake Chas," said Nathaniel as I resurfaced, spitting and spraying for the whole world's benefit. "If it looks plain and safe, your foot will slide on it like a sausage on a greasy pan."

"Yes, thank you, but I hadn't aimed for that one."

"Even worse."

He skipped from stone to stone , with the confidence of a dancer finishing his act. Meanwhile, I pulled myself out on the pointy rocks, trying to avoid the nooks in which crabs had disappeared a second before.

"Since I'm soaked again, I might as well swim the rest of the way."

"These are not waters in which you want to swim," he said.

"Want to scare me with the big bad shark?"

"Don't know if it's big or bad, but you can always stick around a bit longer to see what's under that fin."

I looked to my right, and sure enough, there was a shiny triangle riding the waves.

I was out in a matter of seconds.

"A heads up would have been nice."

"Wrecks attract sharks, it's common knowledge. They remember that once, this very spot was abundant in food. And if you count all the idiots in search of gold with a footing as steady as yours, I would say it's still a reliable source of easy prey for them."

My next jumps were much more thought-out, and therefore, clumsier.

I did however make it to the final reef in one piece.

"I'm having a hard time picturing a person the likes of Lady Winchester hopping along these rocks with ease," I said, once both my feet were firmly set on solid ground.

"That's because you assume a lot," replied Nathaniel. "You forget that everyone on this island has been an active member of a ship crew, and knows their way around waves and shifty floors."

I walked towards the hull of the wreck. Up close, it was indeed impressive.

The bow had a medusa-shaped figurehead that still looked fearsome, even after all the storms and seawater had corroded it. It screamed its defiance to the world, and I could see how a theatrical person like Kathy Winchester should be attracted to it.

"Doesn't this ship have a name?"

"I'm sure it had one, but it was lost with her crew."

"No one gave her one afterwards? 'The Medusa' would sound appropriate, no?"

"You don't name a ship unless you plan to sail it as a captain. It's bad luck."

"Guess I just did. Does that make me captain?"

Nathaniel gave me the look visitors get when they wash their hands in the holy water.

"Very well... I'll take full responsibility for any curse that may come up. Shall we get down to some policing?"

"You're the one paid for making decisions."

The ship was broken in half, creating an opening in its hull. Walking in felt like entering an ancient place of worship.

"Someone built a fire in here!" I said.

Ashes were still smoldering in a rough circle of stones, and the place was stuffy because of the smoke. There weren't many airways up there. It was old and rotten, but it was still a tight ship. Beams could be seen through the smog that had accumulated under the hull. Shapes seemed to move. Parts of the levels had collapsed, making the place look like a multilayered attic after a fire.

"Either we just missed her, or she's hiding somewhere."

Nathaniel raised his head, and sniffed around.

"Whoever was here, it's not her."

"So you can smell tracks as well? They forgot to mention this in your pedigree."

"Lady Winchester always wears heady perfumes. Part of her charm, or however you want to call it."

"You seem to hold her in high esteem as well."

"No, don't... I respect her and all, but... Let's just say the woman's a lot to handle."

"Blimey, my very first case, and I find myself looking for the most intriguing person on the island. Good heavens, what has she done to... Oh no!"
"What?"
"Are you in love with her as well?"
"In... Are you mad?"
"You're blushing!"
"I am *not*!"
"You are blushing like a milk maid at a wine festival!"
"Oh good Lord, come off of your high horses, will you? I saw the way you looked at Selena Montgomery. No please, don't waste your breath trying to deny it, I'm not judging. But the thing is, if you ever get to meet Kathy Winchester, you'll blush as well. Every living being sensitive to the female kind gets 'the feelings' when in her presence, if you catch my drift."
"I'd prefer not to 'catch' anything from you. But I admit she does sound like quite the character. I sure hope we don't find her in the same way we found her late husband."
I looked out the porthole, and saw two boats moored behind the shipwreck.
"Are these the boats meant for the tourists?"
Nathaniel peered.
"Oh yeah... There they are. But I wouldn't risk using them now, after all this time."
He turned around, and started pacing the hull, eyes following imaginary lines on the floor, walls and ceiling.
"Find any clues?" I asked.
"I'm sure I'd be more efficient with some help."
"Nonsense. The only help you need is already there, waiting for you."

73

"Oh, I see. You've solved it already."

"Not at all. But I have a first building block."

"I'm afraid I don't follow."

"Solving a mystery is like building a house. So-called sleuths act as if they were 'discovering' the truth, but there's no such thing. We imagine, create, build, fantasize, and pray to God that it remotely resembles what actually happened."

Nathaniel crouched next to a corner. He rubbed his finger on the floor.

"So you just make up fairy tales in the hopes of nailing the truth?"

"Not exactly. You want to imagine, but within the boundaries of what is given to you."

"Even if you don't have the luxury of time?"

"It's irrelevant. If you rush things, you'll generally be wrong. Almost always. But for instance, if you look here, next to where the fire was, you'll notice wet patches."

He glanced over, and shrugged.

"Nifty. It means a sea creature crawled up here and cooked itself some human for breakfast."

"Could be, could be. But then you'd have wet tracks all over, because it wouldn't have waited to sit down to be all wet, now would it?"

"Right. Maybe it just had too much to drink, and wet itself."

"Oh don't be so daft, will you? Stay with me. The puddle here is still fresh."

"Like I said. Someone came here, lit a fire, and peed themselves."

I took an inquisitive whiff over the tracks.

"Not urine."

"Please, don't ever do that again."

"Hold on, we're not finished yet. If you look closely, you'll notice that the patches are shaped like lumps, which means that someone carried something wet and dropped it in front of the fire to dry."
"I'm starting to see what you meant by making stuff up and seeing what sticks."
"I'm open to all concurring suggestions. If it sounds more plausible, it is welcome."
I crouched next to the glowing embers, and looked into them.
"They do say that staring at the fire can give you interesting insights."
"Fine, I believe you when you say you didn't go to police school."
"The fire tells us someone wet was here to dry up."
"Or to eat."
"No traces of a meal."
"Good heavens, Chas, there's no traces of a crime either. Maybe it was just a poor bloke who was looking for a quiet place and who got scared away by your brutish voice!"
I touched the wet patches, and held my fingers up to my nose.
"Interesting," I said.
"What? That water is wet?"
"Among other things."
He shivered noisily.
"Ugh, you're saying this isn't water. I don't want to know more."
I looked up.
"Ah yes, it makes sense."
"Does it?"
Nathaniel had gone back to the entrance, probably wanting to find something to contradict me with.

"Well, if you look over here, you might find something interesting," I told him.

"What? Blackbeard's head?"

"Didn't Maynard attach it to his ship after killing him?"

"Maynard's a poser. Have you met the man?"

"Can't say I have."

"Well I saw him a couple of times. Scrawny, awkward type. Trying hard to look scary, but failing by a mile. I think he wanted to *be* Blackbeard."

"So that's why he killed him?"

"Maynard never killed Captain Teach, not in a million years. He just grabbed a hairy old head, and played the great sea maverick when he returned to Virginia. Such a waste of space. Which is why Blackbeard's head became a bit of a local joke."

"Interesting. But no, there are no decapitated heads here. If you look in that corner, you'll notice a freshly broken piece of wood."

"Where did you... Oh, you're right. And there's splinters all around. Maybe that was used to build the fire?"

"No, because if you look around carefully, you'll find dents in the hull, fresh dents, as they are still sharp."

Nathaniel searched along the ship's decaying walls, running his fingers on the damp wood.

"Very nice, Chas. I have to give it to you, you do have an eye for small, almost insignificant details."

"I love how your flattery could also be taken as an insult."

"That's *my* charm. It's how I make friends."

"So here's my theory. Solomon Quickbit came here, probably looking for Lady Winchester."

"But she wasn't there."

"Probably not. I say probably, because there was someone else here. Someone who knew, just like us, that Quickbit would be also looking for her. Someone who knew she had been hiding here."

Nathaniel crossed his arms, and looked at me with his head tilted.

"Bear with me," I told him, "I *am* actually going somewhere with this."

"Oh I can see that. It's just I'm not sure if I really want to tag along."

"Humor me. So Quickbit gets here, meets the other person. They have a bit of an argument, maybe even a clash. One of them grabs a piece of wood, probably the other chap, since Quickbit already has a sword. I'm going to bet on an old-fashioned pirate showdown, with the swashing and the buckling."

"If it's going to be a long story, may I suggest you jump to the tasty bits, we have an execution scheduled soon, wouldn't want to be late."

"Almost done. The other one ends up having the upper hand. Quickbit is unconscious. But our man doesn't want him to be just unconscious. He wants him dead. And how do you kill a pirate?"

"Oh, I know that one. Put him in a dark room, and tell him that story?"

"You hang them."

"Aye, that one's only funny among the regulars. But do go on."

"Thank you. So he hangs him, not to make it look like a suicide, but to make it look like an execution."

"And you know that *how*?"

"When you're hanged, you... Produce several kinds of bodily fluids, but none of them are blood."

"I know that."

"And this here, on the floor, is blood."

Credit has to be given where it is due. Nathaniel, annoying and ill-willed as he may be, has no match when it comes to catching up with the rest of the party.

He immediately looked up, and I swear I could almost hear his thinking gears set into place and grind their way to a quick conclusion.

"Bugger. That's Solomon hanging up there?"

"If not, he's a spitting image of the man."

Quickbit's neck was attached to a crudely knotted rope tied around a beam.

"Well that's not good," he commented.

"Perhaps, but at least, it makes him partly innocent."

"And us, a little more guilty."

Chapter 10

"Poor old stormy's dead and gone"

"Are you sure he didn't kill himself?" Nathaniel asked after a bit of pondering. "Out of remorse or something?"

"Oh yes, sure. Better yet, he could have levitated to attach the rope to his neck, and just dropped down."

"Maybe there was a stool, and he kicked it out as he jerked to death."

"And then decided to deal himself a blow to the head just to make sure?"

"Very well, you win. Let's bring him back like this, and say he killed himself out of guilt. We could even forge a letter."

"Your future in the police force looks bright. Yet you forget that there is someone out there that knows we're lying."

"Yes, the actual killer. But so what?"

"I don't know, Nate. It somehow feels wrong to give blackmail material to a murderer."

"What other choice do we have? At least it would buy us some time."

"No. We need to know exactly how he died."

"And how do you plan on learning that? His killer won't tell us, and he sure as hell won't either. Unless you plan on using Wilbur."

"The... Weird magic guy?"
"Yes, the witch doctor, mister Voodoo man himself. He talks to the dead, or so he says."
"He does, now, does he?"
"Just to make things clear, I meant that as a joke."
"You're right, he could definitely tell us how he died!"
"Chas, I think the panic is obscuring your train of thought."
"This way, we'll be that much closer to knowing the truth."
"Yes, along with your horoscope and how bad the next winter will be. Wilbur's a fraud. Granted, he sometimes comes up with tiny pearls of wisdom, but it's like the proverbial broken clock..."
"Not Wilbur. We'll ask actual medicine people!"
"Reine and Félix? They don't talk to the dead."
"There is more than one way to make a dead person talk."
"Oh, they're not going to like this. I suddenly wish you had taken me seriously on my offer to talk to Wilbur."

~

Carrying the body of Solomon Quickbit turned out to be more complicated than I had hoped. Having died quite recently, rigor mortis hadn't started its job. We might as well have been carrying a drunken friend of ours.

Getting him to shore via the pointy rocks and above the shark that had taken a liking to us hadn't been the trickiest part. We could grab him the way we needed to, regardless of decorum, and neither the shark nor Quickbit seemed to mind.

However, these manners would be seriously frowned upon among our fellow *living* humans. We decided to avoid the town as much as possible, going all the way around it, hidden by the trees and bushes, to take Creole Street from the west side.

"And one thing you did not think through either," said Nathaniel while struggling with Quickbit's unruly legs, "is what we are going to do once Reine sends us flying in the streets with our corpse? It's not as if they always wanted to toy around with a stiff pirate. Jesus, how many knees does this man have?"

"Again, it's our only shot. Life gave us a corpse, might as well make the best of it."

"When life sends me a corpse, I'm smart enough to get the message. Which is 'run, run away as fast and as far as possible, you dimwit'!"

"And how do you plan on running? Or did that include swimming?"

"Let me tell you about a fascinating invention called a boat… Great, now we get the mosquitoes."

"Whose boat? Unless you had one hidden up your sleeve? And these mosquitoes are still better than the whole village population trying to dismember us."

"We could have waited for the night, and taken a small rowing boat. No one would have been the wiser."

"And your plan was to paddle away to Louisiana?"

"There are other islands, you know. Hold on, don't walk this way, there's marshes down there. Although getting eaten by a crocodile does sound tempting right now. Ah, speak of the devil!"

Our path was blocked by some large muddy body of water that went up to the town walls.

"What's this?" I asked.

"The marshes I was talking about. Perfect to hide in while waiting for a prey, provided you can hold your breath for long enough, and your body is covered in scales. Not as ideal to walk on with dead Quickbit here, though."

"How far do these marshes go?"

"Erm... All the way to the ocean, I think?"

"So we're stuck."

"Unless we continue through town."

"With him?"

Nathaniel stopped and dropped his half of the body on the floor. I first thought he was about to lose his nerve. It turned out to be worse.

"Besides us and the killer, no one knows he's dead, right?"

"Him being all limp and very pale might tip people off."

"Hold on, here's an idea. We could carry him like a prisoner, you know, keeping his feet on the floor, and if we jerk him around, people might think he's resisting arrest."

"Aren't we a bit too old to be playing puppets?" I asked. Then, as an afterthought: "and not crazy enough to do it with a dead person?"

"Hey, you can't be the only one with the bad ideas. Plus, it may just work. I mean, who in their right mind would be stupid enough to pull such a stunt? Right?"

I was starting to envy the late Solomon Quickbit.

"The quickest way in is through Main Street, where if we do things smoothly, we won't attract too much attention. Then, we make a right on Creole Street, and bam, we're there."

"Or bam, we're dead."

We tied the man's boots to our own to give the illusion of him walking and hid a branch in his back to keep him straight.

"People are staring," I whispered as we entered the crowded streets.

"Of course they are, we do look a bit odd," he whispered back. Then out loud:

"In the name of the Law, Solomon Quickbit, we arrest you!"

I cringed with my whole being, soul and all.

"Stop resisting, and we might go easy on you!" he continued.

All I could do was adopt the meanest possible expression, in the hopes of discouraging anyone from talking to us or even making eye contact.

Lady luck was apparently on our side, since we managed to make it through Main Street, the marketplace, and all the way to the alleyway.

"It's not going to work," said Nathaniel.

"You're not allowed to say such things when you're the one who came up with the plan."

"*Au contraire*, it is my duty to admit failure. This plan was idiotic. It's breaking at the seams, we may as well have painted a smile on his face, stuck a hand up his arse, and made him sing 'Peggy Sue Was a Naughty Girl'."

We made our final turn on Creole Street, and I could see the stairs leading up to Reine and Félix's shop. We only had to walk another forty feet, and we were there.

"Looks like we made it after all," I said. "People are buying it, no one has stopped us so far."

"No one wants to stop a sinking ship. They're just here to watch the disaster."

There's an important thing that has to be said about the streets of New Cayenne. The city was built by the Spanish, as the name indicates, and back then, they had just envisioned it as a temporary thing. They threw in a couple of huts, stomped down a few streets, and called it a day. Later on, as the residents saw their situation morph into something of a more permanent nature, they paved the streets with the enthusiasm and know-how of the wide-eyed amateur.

Well, not so much *paved*, as much as threw rocks around and stuck them together with something that vaguely reminded them of mortar.

It is precisely one of these crudely shaped blocks that violently caught my foot. The rest of my body decided unanimously to respond to such a brutal attack by jumping forward in a way that probably didn't dignify me much.

Quickbit, no longer supported on one side, dove head first, and ended up in a position that would have caused any living being to die quickly and painfully.

"Well if he wasn't entirely dead, we can proudly say that we finished the job," Nathaniel said, embracing the full extent of our epic fiasco.

I looked at the body, and decided to improvise.

"Good Lord, this man needs immediate medical attention!" I shouted.

I looked around as an appeal to witnesses.

"Quick Nate, up to the apothecaries!"

"You're going to hell for this," he whispered.

"I agree," I shouted, "there's no time to waste!"

We hurried up, this time holding him like an actual unconscious person whose feet mysteriously walked in perfect harmony with ours.

I knocked at the door, feeling the gaze of the growing crowd behind us.

"Reine! Félix! It's Charles Gates and Nathaniel! We're here for an emergency!"

"We already told you everything we know!" shouted Reine through the door.

"Yes but this time, we need your services!"

"*Paid* services?" she asked.

"In full!" I answered.

"And with what money?" whispered Nathaniel as Reine unlocked the door.

"One problem at a time, please."

Chapter 11

In Search of a Dead Man's Tale

"What's this?" asked Félix as we laid Quickbit's mortal remains on the floor. His deep baritone voice made everything he said sound stern.

"It's Solomon Quickbit, and we need your help."

"We know very well who this *was*, but we don't do resurrections. *Especially* not with him."

"I'm not asking you for that. What we really could do with, right now, is your knowledge of death."

"The afterlife is not our domain either."

"No, I mean if you could tell us what caused this man's death."

The couple looked at the late Solomon Quickbit.

"I was afraid you were going to ask us that. But that's a coroner's job. We are apothecaries," said Reine.

"Yes, but you know more about the different causes of death than anyone else on this island."

"Why is it so important?"

"It might help us figure out who killed this man."

"Which could incidentally help prove our innocence as well," added Nathaniel.

"That's true!" Reine said. "We heard some interesting stories about you two."

"So you can imagine why we so desperately need your help."

"You know," she said, "your implication with the death of Winchester has made you quite popular among many."

"I've heard that it may even help strengthen your authority in New Cayenne," Félix added.

"I'm sure many will definitely look up to me once I'm hanging from a gallows' pole," I replied. "I'm sorry, but I was hired to uphold the law, and no matter how morally questionable Winchester was, his murder crosses a very big red line. At least for me."

Félix squinted, and scratched the white stubble on his chin.

"As you wish. You said you were willing to pay…?"

"Yes, if I live long enough to receive my salary."

"A wager," Reine noted, an eyebrow raised. "If you win, we all win. But if you lose, we would have worked for free. What makes it worse is that cutting up dead people is not exactly our cup of tea."

Strong willed, and a haggler, I thought.

"I'll give you my whole salary, if it means I live to get paid."

The couple looked at each other, and began another silent council of war.

This time, the change in expressions was so subtle that they just seemed to stare at each other. It felt as if they had already agreed on their answer, but just needed to make sure they weren't getting themselves into more trouble than it was worth.

"We'll do it, Mister Gates," Reine finally said. "But we need to have some guarantee. As you can well imagine, we have been taken advantage of more times than we'd care to remember."

"The fact that we're on an island and that I can't run away isn't enough?" I suggested.

"People always find ways to escape their responsibilities," she said while giving Nathaniel a blank stare.

"I've got something of value," he replied.

Out of his shirt, he produced a book.

"Nate, tell me this is not what I think it is," I told him.

"The Meals and Recipes of Captain Teach," he recited.

"Blackbeard's Cookbook!" exclaimed Reine. "I thought it was in Winchester's possession?"

I considered in all seriousness strangling him at this point. It looked like I was going to be charged for murder regardless. If you're paying for a meal, might as well have dessert.

"Didn't you swear to the mayor's face that you never entered the man's office?" asked Félix.

"And this is the proof that we lied," Nathaniel said.

"So you *did* kill him?"

"No, we are still innocent," he replied. "Let's just say that a regrettable series of circumstances forced us to bend the truth. You can keep this as a guarantee that we will hold our end of the bargain."

"Are you all right, mister Gates?" asked Reine.

My face felt hot, which meant it probably had turned a dark shade of crimson.

"Ungh..." was all that came out from me.

"I'd say he's very surprised I kept incriminating evidence," said Nathaniel, "and he's wondering if he can kill me."

"Can't say I blame him," said Félix. "Very well, it's a deal. We should know what killed this man by the end of the day. Be here around, shall we say sixish?"

88

"Thank you very much," I finally managed. "We'll see you at six."
I tipped my hat, and left the shop. Nathaniel followed me.
"Is there any other thing you've done to incriminate us any further?" I asked once we were outside. "Forgot your shoe at the murder scene? A written confession?"
"Dead men can't read, Chas. He didn't need that book anymore."
"And you didn't bother to think of the consequences?"
"That was *before* we chose to sit back in the waiting room and feign ignorance."
"So you just *conveniently* forgot you had snatched the dead man's book?"
"It's Blackbeard's-"
"I swear if we make it out alive, I'll make you eat it, one page at a time."
"Not the worst possible fate for a cookbook."
"Indeed, there are more painful entryways."

~

The crowd outside had greatly diminished, but some die-hard fans were still waiting for the conclusion of the episode.
"Is he dead?" asked one of them, a little disheveled man with an eye patch.
"It looks dire, but Reine and Félix are doing their best," I answered.
"I don't know what's worse," whispered Nathaniel after we had exited the alley. "Me stealing a book that would take quite a stretch of the imagination to get us hanged, or you making up stories that will definitely come back to bite us in the arse."
"Again, one problem at a time."

"Oh you mean like the last problem, that I managed to solve with that book I shouldn't have stolen?"

"I... Félix and Reine seem like decent folk, I thought..."

"They're decent, but they're far from being idiots. They had their fair share of bamboozlement to know not to trust people like us. Especially since we've become the town's favorite suspects. The last thing they want to do is get mixed up in our affairs."

"And yet they did."

"Because they now have power over us. They know we can't screw them over."

"Which leads to the following question: what made you think it was a good idea?"

"You are right with one thing, they *are* decent people. I probably saved our lives. Some very enthusiastic thank yous are in order."

"I've always had trouble enunciating with a noose around my neck. But anyway, what's done is done."

Once we were far away from our little audience, I came to a halt, and faced my assistant.

"So, since you're full of good ideas, what do you suggest now?"

"Jealousy doesn't look good on you, you know?"

"Jealous of what? Your plan of throwing us to the sharks?"

"It was a good idea and you know it. Now, to answer your question, I suggest we find Lady Winchester. If anyone knows something about her husband's enemies, it should be her."

"A very sensible idea. If only someone had thought of it earlier..."

"You did, granted, along with the idea of dragging a corpse halfway through town. Admit it, pretending he was alive surely was a nice touch..." Nathaniel smiled. "Anyway, enough pointing fingers. Where do we start with Lady Winchester?"

"Drake's Wreck again?" I suggested half-heartedly.

"That would make sense... What about her home?"

"You mean the place where they will cut us in pieces on sight?"

"We are still under the protection of the mayors, aren't we?"

"It is such a thin, almost non-existent protection, that I wouldn't wager a piece of eight on it, let alone our lives."

Nathaniel stared at a distant imaginary point.

"If I were an eccentric rich lady in need of attention, where would I go..."

"Do you think she knows about her husband's death?"

"If she's involved in it, probably."

I closed my eyes and rubbed my forehead, trying to will the hangover to go away.

"Got it!" Nathaniel snapped his fingers.

I looked at him with a mixture of hope and apprehensiveness.

"Why don't we grab a pint at the pub?"

I felt disappointed on both counts. And it showed.

"What?" he griped. "Isn't that what you people do?"

"Us people? The English?"

"No, the police! You know, when the investigation stalls, you drink a few pints, and then you get a brilliant idea!"

"First of all, I trust we had enough to drink for the rest of the week. My head still hurts, and even the idea of looking at a pub makes me nauseous. Two, that's not how it works!"

"It sounded good in the stories."

"What stories? *My people* don't work that way! You do not get drunk to make the story go forward."

"Hey, it worked in Winchester's cellar."

"Correction: it was collateral damage. Plus, had we not been drunk, we could have escaped."

"Very well, how about the fact that in a pub, a lot of people come and go, people that may or may not have seen Lady Winchester, people who talk with the bartender. A bartender we can talk with."
I rolled my eyes. There's nothing worse than a good point that contradicts you.
"A bartender who will gladly answer our questions provided we buy some of his wares."
"Reasoned like a true alcoholic. All right, all right. But just a pint."
Passers-by were still looking at us funny. My guess was that we had become the week's fresh and interesting news.
"Well then," Nathaniel said, "I shall introduce you to Emilio, the proud owner of The Sinking Squid."

Chapter 12

"A bottle of rum, a bottle of gin, a bottle of irish whiskey-o"

The Sinking Squid had once been called just The Squid. It was situated at the very tip of a small pier that oddly stood on a lagoon, where the beams were slowly sinking in the muddy bottom. It had been a bargain for a reason. Emilio realized it a few hours after moving in, but instead of letting that curse discourage him, he turned it into the place's identity.

Thus, the Sinking Squid.

And his little marketing ploy worked. People kept on coming back. You don't want to miss the chance of being the very last customer of the Squid. A fine story to tell the grandchildren, or the pretty ladies at the bar.

"I know it's become a bit of a running joke here, but *do* step lightly," Nate said.

The inside had the typical tavern on the seaside decorations: swords, metal pints, and stuffed shark heads. There were perhaps a few more lifeboats than I would have expected.

"Emilio's an optimist, but he also wouldn't risk letting his customers drown," said Nathaniel, catching my gaze.

"Nate, old pal!" said a man behind the counter with a thin black mustache and long hair painfully pulled back in a small ponytail. "Come to pay your tab?"
"Hello Emilio, I... We are actually here on police business."
"I take it you ran out of evidence against us to trade in for service?" I whispered to him.
"Police business?" asked Emilio. "Oh yes, that's how Boots ended up punishing you!"
He laughed while looking at me, expecting me to join him.
Since I was still new in town, I obliged by groaning with a smile.
"Yes, yes, laugh all you want," said Nathaniel, "but at least I am now a productive member of society."
"Ah, poor Nate, you've sunken really low if you believe that working on the side of the Law is being productive."
Another round of laughter. Other customers had tagged along. Their stares weighed on us threateningly. Pubs had always been the place where a person's reputation was carved with a mix of facts and rumors. A big chunk of my destiny was being decided.
"And you must be Charles Gates, the head of the New Cayenne's Regiments of Armed Police," Emilio told me, his eyes glinting with malicious expectation.
"Does have a nice ring to it," said Nathaniel.
"The N-CRAP?" I snapped back, my smile turning sour.
It finally dawned on my assistant.
"Right..."
"At least crap floats," I hit back. "Which is more than can be said about your business."
It wasn't the best possible comeback, but anger does not bring out the smartest in me.
"Now, now," started Nathaniel, "I think we ought to..."

Emilio burst out laughing, once again.

"Ah, mister Gates. I am very well aware of the shortcomings of my establishment. But instead of letting life use it against me, I embraced it, and wore it like a badge. I suggest you do the same, or else this town will eat you up whole, and spit you out like a hairball."

His hand came out from under the counter, and reached out to me. Since there's nothing worse than a sore loser, I shook it.

"No better way to start over than with a nice fresh pint, what say you?"

"I say that until payday, I'll have to pass."

"Ah, you're barely out of the boat, I'm sure your tab won't mind. Plus this one's on the house."

"Can't say no to that."

He turned around to fill two pints.

"So gentlemen of the police, besides ale, how can I be of assistance?"

He slammed the wooden cups in front of us.

"Because, seeing that you two mustn't have much time to party, I assume you're here to gather some information."

"We wouldn't want to abuse your generosity," said Nathaniel.

"Coming from you, I'd say that's pretty rich, Nate. But who's counting?"

"You are."

"You bet I am."

He winked at me and stood up.

"Just let me take care of my paying customers, and I'll be all yours."

He went to collect empty pints and exchange a few words with his regulars. I did not like the looks we got. My gut feeling told me that before the day was over, I'd regret coming to the Squid.

"I hope the beer is to your liking," said Emilio as he got back to us.

"As always," replied Nathaniel.

"I wasn't talking to you, I know you like it. You'd drink seawater if it had alcohol in it."

"It hits the spot like a cool breeze on a hot day," I said.

"See that Nate? That's how you're supposed to talk if you want to be part of the respectable lot."

He bent over the counter towards me.

"Enough chit chat, let's get down to the business at hand. But make it quick, some ears have a longer reach than others."

"Sounds sensible."

After a quick glance around to discourage listeners, I asked:

"What did you hear about the murder?"

"Which one?"

I raised an eyebrow.

"Oh, people know about Quickbit too. They were mightily entertained to see you two bring him back to life in the streets of New Cayenne."

"All right, all right, let's save him for later. What about the first one?" Emilio leaned in.

"I suggest you have a little talk with Redmayne."

"Her?" I said, looking at Nathaniel. "But, she saved us, and..."

"And where did she send you?"

"She-" I started, then stopped.

She had been the one to urge us to pay Winchester a visit, the very day he was killed.

"Redmayne owes, or rather owed the admiral an awful lot of money. Anyway, that's all I know on the matter."

"Unless we come up with a little something in exchange?"

"Oh no, mister Gates, I said today was free of charge. I am a merchant, but I am also a man of my word."
"Fair enough. Anything on his widow?"
Emilio frowned.
"Let's just say poor old Quickbit would have had interesting things to say about her."
"Yeah, I'm afraid that's a bit of a cold trail."
"This is the Caribbean, mister Gates. In these waters, even the dead can sometimes let out a word or two."

Chapter 13

"Windy weather, boys, stormy weather, boys"

I was surprised to leave the tavern alive and conscious. The sun had set behind the mountains, and the sky's dark blue was turning black.

"Do you think Redmayne would mind if we paid her a visit this late?"

"This isn't London, Chas. Things are not so formal on this side of the pond. *Especially* not on this island."

We walked across town, towards the shipyard.

For some mysterious reason, the streets and alleys felt safer at night. Storm breaker lamps were on almost every wall, giving out a festive and cozy look. Crime was still happening, as sure as rotten eggs smell rotten, but at least it did not prevent you from going on a lazy stroll.

The yard looked like a resting place for monstrous creatures under the moonlight. Hulls of ships lay like sleeping behemoths, while tall masts loomed over us like dragons lurking in the fog.

"Her office is by the wharf. There's a candle burning inside, she's home."

As we walked down the winding road that led to her shack, the candle died, and the door opened.

Following our instincts, Nathaniel and I jumped sideways, as if caught in the middle of a shameful act. We hid behind wooden crates, and waited.

Redmayne stepped out, and locked her door. She looked around, her eyes still adjusting to the darkness. She then walked towards us.

I got Nathaniel's attention by staring at him, then tilted my head in a way that was meant to express the following:

Should we make our presence known and confess that we were hiding, or should we just lay low?

Judging by the empty look on his face, none of it made it through to him.

But then she walked past us, and plan B seemed like the only viable option left. At this point, jumping noisily out of the shadows would not have led to anything fruitful. Plus, she apparently had serious business to attend to, which meant no time to waste with us. All the excuses were lined up.

As her footsteps died away, I saw Nathaniel wave at me. Since we still couldn't whisper without risking being heard, I made the universal "what?" motion. He pointed at her, and made a few gestures that either meant we should follow her, or that he wanted to play crawly spiders on his forearm.

I then answered with the lesser-known "why?" sign, that can sometimes be confused with "what's that smell?"

He got into a full-blown miming sequence that expressed intense restlessness, with a hint of judgment about my mental abilities. Or there was an actual spider taking a stroll in his shirt.

Instead of waiting for me to understand, he darted in Redmayne's direction on tiptoes, while remaining in the shadows.

It was thus that we came to follow her.

~

Luckily, she didn't take any of the main streets, where the lighting would have been too bright for us to remain hidden. But that also meant more chances of tripping over something in the dark. Nate knew these streets like other people's pockets, and managed to follow with ease. I, on the other hand, was constantly one step away from sprawling on the cobblestones.

As I was focusing more on minding my steps rather than hiding, she stopped, and turned around.

Nathaniel, who had been expecting such a thing, danced his way into darker shadows, making himself practically invisible.

I just stood there, frozen, as obvious as a whale on a coffee table. Once your arm is this deep in the cookie jar, it's complicated to come up with a remotely plausible explanation. It did not however stop me from trying.

She looked me dead in the eye, and I found the cleverest thing to say: absolutely nothing. Anything else would have sounded just lame, so why bother?

I just stared back, waiting for her to make her move.

She opened her mouth. I waited. Then she looked up towards the roofs. Finding nothing up there, she turned around, and left.

Nathaniel tiptoed next to me.

"How did you do that?"
"You think she didn't care that I was there?"
"She didn't see you!"
"Not so loud!"
"She looked right through you! Are you *that* insignificant to women?"
"How you made it through life with these bedside manners is nothing short of miraculous."
He frowned.
"Never mind, I guess you're just a lucky bastard. Come on, let's try not to lose her."
Before I could ask him where he thought she was headed, he was gone.
The path she took went through a thickly vegetated part of the island that eventually turned into dead trees and plants.
At one point, she slowed down, and turned her head slowly left and right. She looked nervous, almost scared.
As we matched her pace, I turned to Nathaniel and mimed the question: "where the hell are we?"
He crossed both arms on his chest, hands on his shoulders, eyes closed: the graveyard.
This was proving to be interesting after all. Unless I was mistaken about traditions on this island, people don't go to cemeteries at night to catch up on daily gossip over a cup of tea.
An alarm bell went off in my head.
I stopped Nathaniel, and did the best I could in the dark to tell him the following with only my hands and facial expressions:
"We need to be hiding from the people she's going to meet as well."
The way he tilted his head gave a very convincing illustration of utter puzzlement.

"Someone else hiding," I whispered as low as I could.

"Your *what* is swelling?"

"Who's there?" called Redmayne, "I can hear you."

I slapped the back of my assistant's head. This time, I believe my message was well received.

"Were you followed?" asked a hushed voice somewhere near her. I couldn't tell who it belonged to.

Redmayne gasped.

"Did you have to do this? This place is creepy enough as it is."

"You can never be too safe. Answer me: were you followed?"

"Why do you need to ask such a stupid question? Has anyone in the History of shady meetings ever answered 'uh, come to think of it, maybe'?"

"It's bad luck to play the smartass."

"Since everyone's dying on this island, I may as well go out in style."

"Pirates do love to be cocky, don't they?"

"That's all I have left."

"You'll get your freedom back."

"Of course, provided I do what I'm told."

"Here are your instructions." I heard a papery noise. "Make sure to burn them."

"I may be cocky, but you're being overly dramatic."

"I didn't make it this far by being careless."

"Do you know what people think about you? They-"

"Shhh! I heard a noise."

I looked at Nathaniel who gestured *not me*, then *maybe you?* by pointing a finger back at me and raising an eyebrow.

"We should go. Leave by a different path. And don't forget, only you can make this work. Here's a little thank you in advance."

Something was given, and swiftly put away under a coat.

"Will there be many more deaths?"

"Rome wasn't built in only one kill."

"If you're planning on turning this town into Rome, you may have to kill everyone."

"I suggest you do not find yourself in the vicinity of Town Hall tomorrow. Don't play games, it could make your situation worse than it already is. Now good night. Although I don't expect you to sleep much."

"I doubt *you* will."

Nathaniel and I tried to blend in with the tombstones while trying to catch a glimpse of the mystery guest. We succeeded at the first part, but the latter was a total failure. They both vanished, as if they had never been there.

Nathaniel put his hand on my forearm, his index on his lips.

If he was thinking what I was thinking, he wondered if Redmayne and her associate were still waiting in the dark, in case any potential spy (at your service) gave away their presence by letting their guard down. Either that, or Nate was enjoying our little intimate moment on that warm Caribbean night.

Without any warning sign, he grabbed my hand, stood up, and pulled me to the center of the graveyard.

"Oh Chas, it seems no one's here," he said out loud. So loud I cringed.

"What the hell are you doing?" I hissed.

"No Chas, no, here we can be without fear. Here, you can kiss me, away from all these judging eyes!"

"Are you still drunk?"

"No, Charles, darling, don't push me away. My heart would shatter, and neither Reine nor Félix would be able to mend the broken pieces."

"The…"

A little light went on in my head.

"Yes, the broken pieces. No, I wouldn't want to break your heart, Nate."

"Please call me 'Nate baby' again, where no one can hear us."

"Why sure, Nate… baby. My desire to, er, quench, my thirst for your love is, too precious… Too pure! Yes, too pure. I couldn't do it, in such a place."

"Mind your step, my feisty little canary, it's easy to trip and bash your head in a tombstone. I don't want a stiff for a lover. At least, not entirely…"

"Yes, Nate."

"Nate Baby."

"Nate Baby, I take your point. Why don't we throw caution to the wind, and go back to the office?"

"But I want the wind to caress both our naked bodies."

"Yes, the wind. Our… I'm very sensitive to humidity, you see. Please Nate…"

"Baby."

"Yes, let's go back. Plus I feel like I'm coming up with a headache."

"Typical."

We left using the same road, Nathaniel trying to hold my hand, and me swatting it away.

"I have to say, it is a bit insulting that it took you so much effort to pretend to like me," he said.

Never in my life had I prepared myself for such a complaint.

"Well you did catch me a bit off guard, didn't you?"

"Good grief, if this were real life, I would dump you on the spot! You sounded as enthusiastic as a man being enlisted in the army."

"I had to improvise, and yes, it did not come easy."

"It sounded like pulling teeth. I will always hold this against you."

"Oh come on, don't act as if this really meant something to you."

"Are you assuming it may not?"

I stopped and faced him.

"You made it sound as if that sort of practice was illegal around here."

"And here I was thinking you were a bit on the thick side."

"Aren't pirates liberal about these matters?"

"Yes they are, but not all of them. For beginners, a lot of people on Lilac Hill. And you as well, since you're so keen on changing the subject."

To say I felt awkward would have been quite the understatement.

"Oh, give it a rest, I'm just pulling your leg," he said. "Or I could be pulling something else, who knows? Anyways, I would say it went pretty smoothly up there among the graves, don't you think?"

"You call *that* smooth?"

"You know very well one of them was still there, waiting to see if someone had been spying."

"Yes, I am sure our little performance convinced them of the sincerity of our torrid relationship."

"You're just jealous I came up with the idea. Better to look like hidden lovers than clumsy spies."

"Thanks to you, we may have looked like both."

"You know, all this protesting makes me feel that you don't hate me entirely."

"Oh crap."

"Yes, I know, it's hard to admit how irresistible I can be."

"What time is it?"

"Chas, you're doing it again. Avoiding the subject when the magic is barely budding."

I fumbled my watch out of my vest.

"A quarter over eight!"

"So the night is still young."

"Which is more that can be said about our appointment with Reine and Félix. We were supposed to be there by six!"

"And you plan on ignoring the fact that the mayor is about to be assassinated?"

"What mayor? What does that have to do with anything?"

"They spoke about Town Hall. Who works there? The Queen of Saba?"

"There are *two* mayors there, plus..." my voice trailed off.

"Plus the very zesty Selena Montgomery."

Organizing my thoughts after a day of drowning, drinking, and the two combined, turned out to be a tricky task.

"One of them will be dead by tomorrow, but if we don't know who, there's nothing we can do," I said.

"Let's do a quick detour at Reine and Félix's, and run back down to Town Hall," he suggested.

"Yes, and while we're at it, we can also have a quick smoke up in Bristol, enjoy a little cabaret in Paris, and get drunk in Charles Town."

"With a horse, everything is possible."

"A horse?"

As we walked back within the town walls, Nathaniel led me to a little stable with three steeds on the side of the street.

"Where I come from," I said, "it is highly frowned upon to steal horses".

He gave me a smile that stretched for miles.

"These belong to the town of New Cayenne. You can take any of them, as long as you return it to another station."

"And who pays for this?"

"We all do. You do know about taxes, don't you?"

"Pirates pay taxes?"

"We call it 'sharing the loot'. It does wonders."

He untied a brownish horse, and hopped on its back with ease.

"I suggest you take the one with the dots. He's gentle on beginners."

"You call that dots? He's got patches like a cow."

"Yeah, well Don here is exactly what you can handle right now."

"What about the other?"

Horse number three was grey, and seemed to suit my style a bit more. Nathaniel caught my gaze and snorted.

"Oh, dear heavens, you're considering riding Sally."

"Sally looks decent."

"Sally will eat you up in a single bite, without chewing."

"At least she doesn't look like cattle."

Nathaniel narrowed his eyes.

"You know what? The future of this town may be in jeopardy, but I would sell my own parents to see you have a stroll with Sally. Please, do hop on."

I tried.

In an attempt to imitate Nate's nonchalance, I landed on the other side of the mare, who barely glanced at me.

"Your nether region needs to end up on the horse's back. Preferably with you facing forward."

Grunting, I stood back up. After a few overly cautious tries, I managed to mount Sally.

"All right," I said, "I'm sure I'll get the hang of it as we go."

By the time we got to the apothecary shop, I was hanging on to dear life around Sally's neck, with tufts of her mane up my nostrils.

"You're supposed to sit up straight and use your hips for balance," said Nathaniel.

"Point taken, next time, I'm taking Don."

"That's if Don forgives you."

"I'm sorry, have I offended him in any way?"

"You compared him to a cow."

"Did I say it in horse?"

"Don't underestimate a horse's ability to understand human."

He unmounted with ease, while I just fell like an overripe fruit. We climbed the steps two by two.

Reine and Félix were both seated in a cozy corner of the shop, smoking pipes.

"You're late," said Reine.

"Very sorry, but it's too easy to get sidetracked on this island," I replied.

"Where's the, erm...?" started Nathaniel.

"He's in the cellar, where we keep the medicine cool."

"And I'm guessing you expect us to dispose of it?" I asked.

"What?" Félix cried out. "Heavens no, these are the remains of a human being, albeit not a recommendable one. We've sent for Mister Ezekiel, he should be here in the morning."

"The undertaker," Nathaniel told me, anticipating my question.

"Very well, very well," I said. "So... Anything interesting?"

"The man's very dead," Reine began.

"He sure *felt* that way," said Nathaniel.

"Do not interrupt me, young man! I am not saying this lightly. He was killed a first time, then a second, then a third."

108

"Seems excessive."

"At first, he was poisoned," she explained. "That's what mostly did him in."

"You can see it in his stomach, something like arsenic, quite painful," added Félix.

"But then, and this is an educated guess, he got hit on the head before the heart stopped. For the blood to pour, it needed the heart to be still beating. As for the reason why, it makes no sense. The man was dead, why try to kill him even more? It was unnecessary a second time, let alone a third."

"Right," I said. "And I guess the third one was the hanging."

"This goes beyond any logic. Two would have sufficed if the goal was to conceal the poison. But the three together?"

"One might even call this *overkill*," said Nathaniel, who looked as smug as his joke was bad.

But I wasn't in the mood for smiling.

There is such a thing as too many clues. With only one, especially a benign one, you can reconstruct a big chunk of the case. Two, confusion starts to seep in. But with all these elements, about anything was possible. Except making proper sense of it.

"And where can you get this... Poison?" I asked, a bit embarrassed by the question's unavoidable undertones.

"Not from us," Reine said dryly. "We are in the business of making people better, unlike *some* others."

"Speaking of which," Félix commented, "you may learn some interesting things from our local witch doctor, Wilbur."

"Ah, the voodoo man?"

"He doesn't even deserve that title," Reine said.

They both made a face usually associated with the discovery of rotten vegetables.

"Thank you Reine, thank you Félix," I said, standing up.

"I'm afraid our help is not what you had hoped for," said Félix.

"Quite the opposite. Thanks to you, we now know the assassin has done quite the job of hiding their tracks."

"Or that they're unable to make up their mind," Nathaniel said.

"That last part," I remembered, "the hanging. It looks more like a message. A direct threat against pirates."

"But then why the first two?" asked Reine. "Hanging is a pretty efficient way in its own right, if you ask me. And it sends the message."

"Well I can tell you would have made a much more efficient and level-minded killer, Madame Reine."

She laughed, even though I had expected a scowl.

"The day I start killing people," she said, "I won't even try to hide it".

"Right," interrupted Félix, a bit embarrassed, "but there's another annoying thing I had forgotten."

He cleared his throat, and looked at me.

"The wound on the head is not deadly. Bloody, for sure, but then again any nick on the scalp turns quickly into a bloodbath. *That* wasn't meant to kill."

"Maybe... The poison wasn't working, the killer overreacted, knocked him out, then hung him for good measure?"

Félix rubbed his mustache.

"Plausible... Then your killer would have been in some kind of panic..."

"Then that's definitely not me," said Reine.

"If we weren't so far in your debt," Nathaniel said, "I'd be very tempted to say that you sound mightily suspicious, Madame Reine."

"Don't we all?" she replied, her voice suddenly serious. "On this island, almost everyone has a good reason to kill. It's all so fragile. Our little republic of pirates could shatter at any moment."

I looked at Nathaniel with one of those meaningful stares, which was immediately picked up by the couple.

"I say follow your hunch boys," said Félix. "This place may not be much to you, but it's the only one we have where we can live as free people. If you can help it stay afloat, we would be grateful."

"And all my friends thought I was going for a cozy retreat in the Caribbean..." I said.

I bowed, and made for the door.

"Oh, one last thing," I said, clearing my throat. "Would it be crazy to think that, perhaps, the same thing was done to Winchester? Poison first, then stabbing?"

"Why, do you plan on bringing us his body as well?" asked Reine.

"It's becoming unreasonable, isn't it?"

"We'll go with the undertaker, and give the old bastard a look," Félix said.

"Guess I'll owe you two of my salaries then."

"We would be willing to do it for free if you carried the Admiral through town the same way you did with Quickbit."

"I'd rather you took my money."

They laughed.

Chapter 14

"Those who kill by the sword…"

Nathaniel walked out a minute after I had been waiting in the street.
"What were you doing up there? Finally got your private ointments?"
"Pipe down, will you? I was there for barely a minute!"
"Well a minute might just mean the difference between a happy ending and a short drop with a quick stop."
"All right, all right, I'm sorry... So, what's the plan? Confront Redmayne?"
"I think we need to know where that poison came from first."
"Wouldn't talking to an actual suspect with motives be more productive? Oh, you want to see my 'told you so' dance once again, I get it."
"I was wrong once, you can get off of your high horses. And speaking of which, going to Wilbur's shouldn't take too long."
"Not the way *you're* riding."
"It's a learning curve."

~

The 'learning curve' felt more like a downward spiral.

"Chas, we've been through this, you're supposed to be *on* the horse."

"Really! And to think I enjoyed riding sideways!"

"Careful, Sally doesn't respond well to sarcasm."

"Got it. Next time, I'll go for brutal honesty."

Wilbur's house was on a strange rock formation between Queen Anne street, properly lit at night, and the Broken Light District, unsurprisingly shadier, even during the day.

"That's Wilbur down to a bloody 'T'," said Nathaniel. "Right between the mildly poor, and the mildly rich."

"Why not go for the extremes? It would make for a stronger statement."

"There's no direct border between those. Plus, there's more money in the middle."

The house was an oversized barrel of wine revamped to look like a house in the shape of a skull. The results were more along the lines of a misshapen wooden crate with holes in it.

There was a wobbly lamp on what was meant to be his porch.

"Hey Wilbur!" called Nathaniel. "You home?"

No answer. But it felt like we had woken up an ancient sea monster.

"I may or may not have food," he teased.

"What time is it?" said a sepulchral voice.

"A spiritual fellow like you cares not for such trivial matters!"

"Spiritual my foot!"

Something crawled out of the hut.

It had a lot of hair. Unkempt, dirty hair. Too much hair for a human being.

Then I realized it wasn't human. At least, it wasn't *all* human.

Some of it belonged to some furry animal that had been gruesomely killed, and reconverted into a clothing accessory that covered its proprietor like a rudimentary cloak.

And it had horns.

The hairiness made up for the man's light fuzz on the chin.

"Who dares disturb the Witch Doctor in his sleep?" he said in an overly ominous voice.

"We're the..." I started, then hesitated.

"Go ahead," said Nate. "Like Emilio said, own it."

"The New Cayenne Regiment of Armed Police."

Wilbur frowned, revealing new lines on his face, and stroked his chin with his thumb. The man was somewhere between his thirties and his seventies and had the wrinkles you get when you try to look thunderous all the time.

And when you drink a lot too.

"The New CRAP?" he finally figured out.

"Yes, I feel it does give a sense of what's coming to people when they get on our wrong side."

Wilbur sunk back into pondering, while Nathaniel gave me a raised eyebrow.

"The side that gives out crap?"

"Exactly. Now we were wondering if you could answer some questions."

"At this time of night?"

"First of all, it's an emergency, and second, it's barely eight in the evening!"

He eyed me with a mild degree of malevolence.

"Wisdom rests whenever it deems it suitable to."

He yawned, exposing an unexpected full set of ivory white teeth.

"You said you had food?"

"Not right now," Nathaniel answered, "but I could get you some."

"Nature abhors a trickster."

"So," I said, "rumor has it that you sell poisons?"

The malevolence went from mild to intense in a flinch.

"Depends. Who's asking?"

"My apologies. The name's Charles Gates."

"Gates, hmm? Which ones? The Gates to Heaven? Or the other ones? I sense some dark things in your aura."

"Yes, my aura has had too much booze and not enough rest lately. You could however unburden it by answering my question."

The man came entirely out of his hut, and stood up, stretching. The amount of bones cracking made me wince.

"Very well, Gates. I do sell poisons, among many, many other things."

"Is that so?"

"But poisons are not necessarily used to kill. In small quantities, any deadly concoction can strengthen, lengthen..."

"Yes, I'm talking about plain arsenic. Something typically deadly."

"Is it illegal to want to kill rats?"

"With arsenic?" asked Nathaniel. "How big are the rats?"

"I respect the confidentiality of my customer's needs."

"Fair enough," I told him. "But now, there's been a murder by poison, and if it gets known that what you sell may have been the cause..."

"Ah, a threat?"

"A friendly warning. You are obviously a reputable..."

He waited for the word I was going to use.

"Healer," Nathaniel suggested.

"Yes, healer, thank you. I will undoubtedly require your services one day or another. But right now, you have information that is quite relevant to me, and more importantly, to justice."

"Then buy something from me."

My stiff upper lip faltered a little.

"Are you making us pay for information?"

"Not at all, not at all, Gates. I am not withholding anything. I will give you the information. But if it involves a little transaction, I will give it *gladly*."

Nathaniel smirked.

"We are in a little bit of a hurry, you know, matter of life and death, that sort of thing..."

"I have *exactly* what you need!"

"You mean besides the information?"

"My friend, you expect too much of this information. What you need, in order to illuminate the dark skies of your destiny, is *this*!"

He brought out from under his dead animal a phial, with something that sloshed unenthusiastically inside.

"And this is...?"

"My latest *Bad Juju Away Elixir 1800*!"

To his great disappointment, I didn't look as excited as he expected me to be.

"It will lighten up your mood, re-grow your hair, strengthen your appetite, diminish what needs diminishing, and lengthen what needs lengthening."

He winked at me.

"Quite frankly..." I started.

"And it's lead-free! Usually at ten pieces of eight, exceptionally today at six!"

"Six? That's-"

"I'll make it five for you, call it a special friend's price."

I took an expression of pained regret.

"The thing is, I am quite light on money for the time being."

"Nonsense, nonsense, *the house accepts credit!*"

He said that last part extra loud, for all the neighbors to hear. Then he added, in the verbal equivalent of the fine print:

"For a small fee of one extra piece of eight per day."

He slipped the bottle in my coat pocket.

"A pleasure doing business, Gates. Mark my words, before you know it, you'll be coming back for more!"

I opened my mouth, but decided against it. There were more urgent things than talking myself out of a con.

"Very well, you'll get paid, with the late fees. Now, about that information?"

"A person *did* buy cyanide from me."

"Didn't I say arsenic?"

"Yes, yes, I meant arsenic."

"Didn't Félix say cyanide?" asked Nathaniel.

"Do you want the bloody information or not?"

"Well, it matters if it's not the poison we're looking for."

"The lady asked for a strong poison," he said.

"Ah so it was a lady. And her name is?"

"I don't know. She was tall, wore a hood, and it was dark. But I distinctly saw well-groomed locks of hair."

My face grew as long as a cloudy day.

"I'm sorry to say that your fix-it-all potion is more exciting than this piece of information."

"Well, that's all I can give you. I even made her pay extra for being so secretive."

"Well obviously, you don't purchase a deadly poison in the same manner you buy cucumbers do you?"
Nathaniel was smiling to no one in particular.
"Oh bugger off," I told him.

Chapter 15
"Way-hay up she rises"

"It could be anyone," I told Nathaniel while struggling to remain on Sally's back. "I know Redmayne seems like the ideal suspect, but she's not alone in this."
"Call me crazy, but I think she likes you."
I almost fell off.
"What? What makes you say that?"
"She's patient with you, seems to enjoy your touch... And when you climb on her, she no longer tries to catapult you to the next island. What's wrong? You seem disappointed."
"No, but I'd like it if you stuck to the subject at hand."
"You thought I was talking about... Oh no, Chas, not her. Redmayne hates everyone, boys and girls alike. She wants to be left alone with her ships. And preferably without debt."
"Yes, but would she kill for that?"
"We just need to go and ask her."
I hesitated.
"I was right after all, *twice* today," he added.
"One and a half. We still have to see how the confrontation with her would turn out, and when you think of it, Wilbur wasn't a complete waste of time."

"True, you got yourself one of his miracle elixirs that you'll end up paying full price. Twice."

My hand went to the pocket where the phial was.

"We also know that it was a woman who bought the poison."

"Yes, Redmayne. We would have known it by going straight to her as well. But hey, now you can 'shorten what needs shortening, and lengthen what needs lengthening', right?"

"Do you actually believe that?"

"It probably has *some* virtues, like making you feel a bit drunk, and seeing things in the mirror, but I'm afraid that's it."

"No, do you really think that by just showing up at her place and accusing her point blank, she will just break down and confess to everything?"

"Surely at police school they taught you ways to make people talk? Or are you expecting me to solve this one as well?"

"I never went to... Anyway, yes, there are methods to make people talk, but none of them involves knocking at their door in the evening and just asking them. Especially not the two of us."

"I beg to differ. If some strange, mean-looking thugs came up to my house at night, I'd feel inclined to talk."

"*Mean-looking thugs*, eh?"

Nathaniel grimaced.

"I agree that we may be lacking in the 'mean' department, I'll give you that. But in my opinion, given the right mood, there's always a way."

I stared ahead.

"You know," I said, "as much as I hate to say it, you might be onto something, there."

He beamed.

"Well you sure know how to make a lady feel special. Almost feels like a promotion," he said.

"Unfortunately, it wouldn't involve you."

He narrowed his eyes.

"You know, when I said you could make a lady feel special, I didn't mean it as an actual compliment."

"Well, I *am* following your advice, aren't I?"

"Oh I see. You want to be all alone with her, work out the old policeman charm on her, don't you?"

"No charm there, just... Trying to appeal to, you know..."

"Her better nature? She's a pirate, not a philanthropist."

"Yes, but I have a lever. She needs something."

"Money to pay her debts. Did you suddenly get rich in the last five minutes?"

"No, but I'm sure I can find a way to make myself useful."

"Care to elaborate?"

"No, I feel it's bad luck to reveal my plans to you."

"You can be very petty, you know that?"

"Hey, when amongst pirates, like you said, right? And now that I think of it, it would be more fruitful to go separate ways, don't you think? I take care of the Redmayne situation, while you..."

"Go hold the candle elsewhere?"

"If I didn't know better, I'd say you're obsessed with things that pertain to intimacy."

"Who isn't? And what's that important other thing I should take care of?"

"For one thing, you could go see what is happening at Town Hall."

"Sending me off to the front line, are you?"

"We could always switch, I'm sure Redmayne would be overjoyed with the idea of confiding in you..."

"When this is over, you'll *wish* I had chosen Redmayne. Let's meet up at the Sinking Squid afterwards. You'll definitely need a drink. Yes, another one."

He galloped away.

~

Thanks to Sally, my arrival at the shipyard was anything but inconspicuous. I was huffing and puffing like an old kettle forgotten on the fire.

This time, all the lamps in the yard were brightly lit, like for a carnival. The different colors of wood came to life, and it wouldn't have felt creepy at all, hadn't it been for the complete silence in which everything was frozen.

Her shack, however, had all its lights turned off.

"And what brings you at such an hour?"

Redmayne's voice came from somewhere above me. I struggled to find something smart to say.

"Good heavens Gates," she added, "this is *not* how God intended us to ride horses!"

"It's like everything I do on this island, I'm still in the trial-and-error phase."

"There are mistakes from which you can learn, and there are the ones you only get to make once. I suggest you learn the difference. Quick."

"Are you referring to me getting attached to an underwater beam?"

"I am referring to you coming unannounced to my house at night."

I suddenly felt the eye of a pistol on me.

"I am still an officer of the law."

"Not to me, not yet. Over here, you have to earn your place. This is not London, or Paris, or one of your fancy cities with a king, where any fool with a title can act as he pleases."

"I fully understand, and I came here to talk."

"You expect me to trust you just like that?"

"Since I owe you my life, being truthful is the least I can do."

She said nothing.

Instead, I heard shuffling sounds, like cloth on wood. She then hopped from her roof into the light.

"Come in. And try not to kill yourself while unmounting."

Chapter 16

"Way-hay up she rises" part 2

I followed her in.

She had lit a candle on her kitchen table, but was nowhere to be seen.

"Hello?" I called.

"Have a seat. I'd rather remain in the shadows, if you don't mind."

"Why all the precautions?"

"By now, haven't you learned that you can never be too careful around here?"

I sat down, with my back to where her voice came from.

"So, Mister Gates, what can I do for you? Again?"

"Yes, I know I'm already in your debt, and I can't be thankful enough. You saved my life, and you gave me a lead in this investigation, the latter being the most valuable in my line of work."

"I heard things didn't go as expected at Winchester's?"

"Through no fault of yours, mind you. Had he not been dead, I'm sure persuading him of our good intentions would have been much easier."

I tried to listen to her think, but she seemed to be able to control even her breathing.

"Luckily, the mayor and his replacement seem to trust us, so we won't be hanging at the harbor just yet," I said.

It could have been my imagination, but I felt her shift a little.

"You think I deliberately sent you there, knowing he was dead."

"I'm sorry, what?"

"Stop playing dumb with me. Men usually think themselves smarter than they really are, which makes them insufferable. But what you're doing is actually worse."

"Oh, so I'm supposed to think you knew Winchester was about to be killed?" I asked.

No immediate answer, and that meant a lot. I pushed my bluff a bit further.

"Unless you managed to run up the hill past us, climb up his window, and stab him just before we were asked to sit in his waiting room?"

"What game are you playing?"

"Stupid, I guess?"

She jumped out of the shadows, and planted a knife through the table, between me and the candle. She then sat on the other side and crossed her arms.

"You think you know things, and you intend to scare me. Use that big brain of yours, and guess what that little plan can do to your health."

"I'm guessing anyone trying to outsmart you wouldn't make it to the end of their sentence?"

"I like to think I would allow for the whole conversation to happen, but you seem to know me better. So try again. You were about to tell me your true intentions."

This was like a game of cards. I had eliminated a few possible hands, but I was riding high on the wave of assumptions. On the bright side, if I was to crash, I would crash hard.

"Someone's blackmailing you."

"And yet somehow, they live?"

"I guess they're more talented than I am."

She smiled, and started tapping her fingers on the table.

"That's more like it."

"My modesty?"

"Your sense of superiority. It shines through your so-called modesty."

"I... You know what? I apologize."

"You apologize? For what?"

"I followed you earlier tonight."

She stopped smiling.

"Go on."

"I... We, Nathaniel and I, we wanted to talk to you. But then we saw you walk out, and decided to remain hidden. I'm sorry to say it, but we followed you. All the way."

She stared at the candle.

"I am very sorry," I said, trying to sound as sincere as I felt. "But I want to help."

She said nothing, but her features had tensed.

"Someone has put you in a difficult situation, I want to say an impossible one... I guess what I'm trying to say is, there's a way out."

"And you're my way out?"

"Not in a *knight in shining armor* way, I'm afraid, however I promise I can be resourceful."

A corner of her mouth went up.

"I'm not a trusting person," she said, "and that's for starters. But I'm sure you can very well understand that right now, things are not looking good for you."

"Oh I fully understand, and I don't expect you to just..."

"You followed me. In the dark. You could have made your presence known, walked up to me. You could have acted like the honest person you pretend to be."

"In my line of work, I also have to be careful. Plus I don't trust people easily either."

"Don't hide behind your work. You followed me. That's what thieves do. That's what murderers do. And you spied."

If Nathaniel was ever to hear about this conversation, I would have to thoroughly edit it to avoid becoming the butt of all jokes for years to come.

"Now that you mention it, at one point, I did hear something," she said.

Her eyes rolled towards the ceiling, as if looking for inspiration.

"I knew it, I felt it, I could have sworn someone was behind me. I even turned around."

I must have looked like a child caught with a box of matches in front of a burning house.

"I looked down the street, and there you were, standing, just standing, with the expression of a duck staring at an oncoming galleon."

My stomach felt full of bricks.

"I was about to talk to you," she continued, "but seeing how motionless you remained, I realized that you thought I hadn't seen you," she said.

She stood up.

"You are all so easily fooled with the illusion of your abilities. Always ready to believe you're so amazingly skilled. I mean, I *stared* at you, face to face. And you really think I did not see you?"
I almost preferred the idea of Nathaniel having a good laugh.
"You see, mister Gates, I *did* have a secret meeting, but when I saw you were following me in such a clumsy manner, I thought I'd have a bit of fun. At your expense."
I was biting my cheek.
"Because unlike you, I can *whisper*. I explained the situation to my partner, we improvised, and you weren't the wiser. By the way, I loved your little act with Nate at the end. Very cute. I could have the whole town roaring with laughter for weeks with that story."
I smiled.
"I guess that's fair. Albeit a bit odd to choose to have fun in such a situation."
"It's never a bad time to have a good time, mister Gates."
She opened a cupboard, and took out a bottle.
"Wine?" she asked.
"I'm not sure I'm ready for that kind of good time."
She filled two glasses, and handed them to me.
"Why both?" I asked.
"In case I poisoned one of them."
"Maybe you poisoned both?"
She sat down.
"What brought you to New Cayenne, mister Gates?"
I took the glass in her right hand.
"I got tired of the rain, I guess."
"That's it? You left your entire life behind because of the weather?"
"Is that so outlandish?"

"Spain has nice weather. So does Italy. In fact, there are plenty of sunny places that aren't worlds away from where you were born."

"I guess I got tired of the old world."

"Maybe you got tired of crowned heads as well?"

I looked at her, then gently spun my glass and watched the wine swirl.

"The people who live on this island are running away from those crowns and their thugs," she said. "Did you do something to anger someone important?"

"More than just some*one*. But I didn't have to run."

"Or maybe you were kicked out. They let you live if you disappeared from their world."

I sniffed.

"So now, you're the one leading the investigation?" I scoffed.

"Well first of all, anyone who cares to ask knows that it rains here as well. And much, much harder."

"True."

She was playing with me, that much was obvious. But she hadn't kicked me out. Better yet, I was still alive, able to speak and ask questions. As long as she thought I knew something, I was safe. I just needed to guess what I was supposed to know.

"Tell you what," I said, "why don't I let you in on one of my secrets, and you let me in on one of yours?"

"What makes you think I have secrets?"

"Oh come on, you went out at night to meet someone in a cemetery. I mean, granted, you managed to pull my leg, well done. But I think I'm right in saying you weren't out there to discuss a client's ideas on the length of his main mast."

"Ah, you got me there."

She laughed. It sounded fake.

I laughed too. And made it sound even faker.

"But according to your deal," she added, "*you* are supposed to go first."

"And I shall honor my end of the bargain."

She hadn't touched the wine, so I pretended to have forgotten about it. She had apparently opted for that old tried and proven trick, and I didn't plan to fall for it.

What's good for the Borgias is definitely not ideal for others.

"I may or may not have gotten a bit too close to someone's wife."

"How important was that someone?"

"Important enough."

"And how close did you get?" she asked, leaning in.

"Close enough."

"How come you didn't end up in jail?"

"Ah," I sighed, "I had done that family several great favors, so they felt they owed me some mercy."

"Such a sweet story. Probably not true, but sweet."

"Would swearing on my father's grave make any difference?"

"Easiest kind of oath, unless the dead decide to come back to reclaim their dues. Actual names, on the other hand, would make it more believable."

"I'm afraid we're too early in our relationship for me to reveal that much."

"Very well. I guess it's my turn now."

She looked at my cup.

"You still don't trust me do you?"

"Oh right, the wine..."

She grabbed her glass, took a sip, and then did the same with mine.

"There. Reassured?"

"Interesting. I guess this means you're not the one who poisoned Quickbit."

"He was *poisoned*?"

She sprang up. Both glasses fell and shattered on the floor."

"That's impossible!"

It felt as if all the cards had gotten back in my hands. The whole deck. At last, one of my bluffs had worked.

"Is there something wrong?"

She put her hand to her chest, as if to examine herself.

"How do you know it was poison?" she asked.

"How do *you* know it was supposed to be something else?" I asked back.

She looked aghast, her terrified eyes locked on mine.

"I am not playing, how do you know it was poison?"

"We had his body examined by Reine and Félix..."

"Oh no, oh no, oh..."

She ran to the cupboard, took out a glass bottle that seemed to be filled with milk, and started drinking.

"Clarisse? What's happening?"

"I stabbed Solomon in the head and he died almost instantly! I thought it was too quick, what an idiot, what an *idiot*!"

She gulped down the bottle, bent over, and started retching. I ran to her.

"Are you sure you drank poison?"

"I was told I'd probably die the way he did, and laughed it off! Oh God!"

She hugged her stomach, and started crying.

"The bottle..." she managed, "it was part of the payment, oh God!"

Her crying turned into screams of pain. I crouched in front of her and held her shoulders.

"We must go to the apothecaries! Now!"
"It's too late!" she said, before collapsing, still screaming.
"Who gave you this bottle?" I asked, panicking with guilt.
The only answer I got was an agonizing howling. Then she passed out.
"Damn it!" I shouted.
I picked her up, and saw something drop on the floor: a folded piece of paper. I picked it up, and put it away in a pocket.

~

Sally looked at me expectantly.
"All right girl, I really need you to cooperate."
I slung Redmayne on her back, and fumbled with the rope. The knot was too tight, it was taking forever. I took my knife out, and slashed it. Sally remained unfazed.
I mounted in the least elegant way, right against Redmayne's unconscious body.
"Come on, let's go girl!"
I couldn't have wished for worse, with my non-existing riding skills and lack of level-headedness. But Sally seemed to understand exactly what was happening, and stepped up to the task.
As we left, I realized I couldn't for the life of me remember the way to Reine and Félix's shop. I had only been there twice. The first time, I hadn't been paying attention, and the second, I was too busy playing puppets with a dead Quickbit.
Sally, who was as smart as she was temperamental, got us there. The street lamps got fewer, the houses got smaller, and I recognized the road, then the alley to the shop.

"Good girl! I promise I'll get you full cargos of carrots, or whatever it is that rocks your boat!"

I jumped down, and carried Redmayne up the stairs in a way my knees didn't appreciate much.

There was a note pinned to the door.

"Out to the undertaker's," it said.

I cursed loud enough for the whole town to hear me. I had only two options left.

First, I could break in, and look for a phial that said 'arsenic antidote'. But the actual

antidote had probably a more scientific name, which I wouldn't have been able to tell from an even deadlier poison.

Or, I could go to the undertaker's shop, but with absolutely zero clue as to where it was.

I put Redmayne back on Sally, and took the road again. If a mistake was to be made, I felt better leaving it to the professionals. It was cowardly, but I was running out of damns to give.

However, I did blame myself for asking Reine and Félix to go examine Winchester. Each and every one of my decisions seemed to have been made for the worse:

Going to Winchester's first instead of the mayor.

Spying on Redmayne instead of looking for Lady Winchester.

Sending Nathaniel away when I still couldn't find my way in town.

"Sally, you wouldn't happen to know where the undertaker lives?"

She barely looked at me.

"Worth a shot."

Wilbur would have known, but by the time I got him out of his hut, it would have been too late for Redmayne.

So I decided to sacrifice the little self-respect I had left and asked myself: "what would Nathaniel do?"

The answer came to me with my assistant's know-it-all attitude: "where do undertakers usually work?"
"Hi-yo, Sally! To the graveyard!"
We trotted away.

Chapter 17
Death Can Be Such a Pain

I almost missed it.

I was so intent on trying to find a pulse on Redmayne over the horse's clippity-clop, that I nearly went by Ye Olde Funeral Services ("being at your very worst doesn't mean you cannot look your very best") without seeing it.

The parlor wasn't next to the cemetery. It wasn't even close.

One could have argued that it was *on the way* to the graveyard, but in that respect, all the roads in town were on the way to the graveyard.

It was right off the marketplace.

There were coffins on the front yard as a display, with skeletons giving passers-by a thumbs up. A sense of humor was most certainly a vital thing in such a profession, but perhaps this one was having a bit too much fun outside the borders of sanity.

I jumped off Sally, realized too late that it was not something I had mastered yet, and fell in one of the caskets, damaging its grinning tenant beyond repair.

Sally whinnied.

"Sure, laugh away, why don't you."

I grabbed Redmayne, ran to the door, and hit it like a tax collector taking things personally.

"In the name of the Law, I require your services!"

I saw faces appear in the neighboring windows, but couldn't care less. There was still a chance for her to make it. A very fragile one, but I was placing all my bets on it.

The door opened.

A man, tall and hunched like a dead willow, loomed out.

"Terribly sorry, but I have an emergency! Are Reine and Félix here?"

As I asked that question, I felt a pang of panic. What if the answer had been 'no'? It would have been over. I didn't know how poisons worked, but my guess was that galloping around town was not the best way to treat them.

"You're that policeman," he said, with a voice that confirmed that he accompanied people to their grave, and probably beyond. "Business has been booming since your arrival."

"Yes, you're welcome, but..."

"They're here, in my basement. Although I'm not sure about Captain Redmayne's emergency. People don't tend to get better in this house."

"Well there's always a first time."

He led me to his basement, much faster than his demeanor would have suggested. I found my favorite apothecaries gathered around a table on which Winchester's mortal remains lay.

"What is..." started Félix. "What, you killed her as well?"

"No, she drank poison, and I figured you could help."

They pushed the Admiral to the edge of the table to make some space.

"What poison?" asked Reine.

"I'm going to go with my gut feeling and say arsenic?"
"What were the symptoms?"
I drew a blank. Suddenly I felt very tired. She was going to die because of a last-minute brain malfunction.
"She... Was in pain, in great pain."
"Pain where?"
"In her stomach, I suppose. And she threw up. And then she screamed."
"It does sound like arsenic," said Félix. "When did she ingest it?"
"Well... How long does it take to ride a horse from the shipyard to your shop, and then all the way here?"
They looked unimpressed.
"That long ago."
"That's not very good," said Reine. "From what you're saying, she ingested a harmful dose. And we don't have our potions."
She looked at the undertaker.
"Mark, do you have any potassium?"
Mark the undertaker, I thought.
"Not the kind made for the living," he answered.
"If it's solid," said Félix, "just bring it with a glass of water."
Mark vanished as if in a magic show. I blinked. One second he was there, among us, and the next, he was just gone. The man was a living metaphor of death.
"How did that happen?" Félix asked me.
"No idea, you tell me... Oh with her, sorry. She drank wine, and she started screaming."
"That's not just arsenic, it must have been spiked," he said. "But the potassium may help slow things down until we get back to our shop."

Mark came back with a glass of water, and what seemed to be a rock in it.

"Ah, you use *that* kind of potassium," Reine said. "What is it for? Preservation of the organs?"

"It makes the eyes shine," Mark replied.

"But don't you people close them for the funeral?" I asked.

"We do. But in the same way that you can hear a smile in the voice, shiny eyes can be felt through the eyelids. Makes them look gently asleep."

Reine took a syringe from the wall.

"Is this clean?"

"A clean environment makes for a healthy-looking cadaver."

"A 'yes' would have sufficed."

She filled it with water from the glass, and proceeded to administer it slowly through Redmayne's lips. They were blue.

"Mark, I know we're asking for a lot," Reine said, "but we're going to need your carriage to bring her back to our shop. We'll get it back to you as fast as possible."

"In my world, no one is ever in a hurry."

"Thank you, Mark," Félix said.

"Yes, thank you," I added.

"Does it mean that much to you?" the apothecary asked me.

"I think I just want this to be over without any additional corpses. And I'm tired."

He put his hand on her neck, right underneath her jaw, and frowned at me.

"I'm afraid her chances are slim. Just help us bring her to the carriage. If we're lucky, she won't have to ride it back here."

Her body was still soft, and smelled of sweat, wine, and dried flowers.

As they sat at the reins, my police instincts kicked back in.

"Did you find out anything about Winchester?"

"You were right, he had ingested something that resembles arsenic. His heart had stopped before the sword went through him, which is why so little blood was spilled."

I felt selfishly glad to have been right for once.

Félix shouted something in French to the horses, and the carriage took off.

"You haven't seen Nathaniel lately by any chance?" I shouted.

"Happy to say I haven't," replied Félix, before disappearing around the corner.

"Guess he finally ran away," I said to Sally. She snorted lazily. The sun was starting to come up. The darkness was fading away, if only temporarily.

"I strongly believe everything will be better after a good nap, don't you think?"

The ride back home had its ups and downs. Sometimes, I was up on the horse's back. The others, I was down with my head in the gutter.

The little honeymoon Sally and I had shared was officially over, but I felt I was starting to get the hang of this lawless merry-go-round.

~

It turns out there was a horse station near my office. It was empty and forlorn, but it had what I needed to park Sally there.

Once all was said and done, I finally walked to the door for some well-deserved rest.

Something was sticking from underneath it, on the non-existent welcome mat. I picked it up.

It was a note.

"Big trouble in Town Hall, as expected. Meet me at Drake's Wreck. Don't let anyone see you. Absolutely no one. Be quick. Even quicker. N."

"So you can read *and* write," I said to the note.

The whole Town Hall story had supposedly been made up to lead us down a wild goose chase. But then again, Redmayne had been poisoned, and had confessed to stabbing Quickbit in the head. This goose was not so wild after all.

With a long sigh, I decided that my bed would have to wait.

Chapter 18

A Quick Stroll on the Wild Side

To avoid attracting too much attention, I chose the jungle to the east. All I had to do was reach the beach, and the wreck would be within a quick walk.

That part of the island was mostly made of palm trees, giant flowers, and rabid mosquitoes. A big fat lot of bloodthirsty mosquitoes.

At first, I regretted not taking Sally with me, but as it turned out, it would have been a deadly mistake for her.

Swamps are a fascinating geographical phenomenon. You could see them as the unlucky lovechild of solid ground and the sea. Unlucky, because instead of getting the best of both worlds, like coolness, stability, and a rich ecosystem likely to feed many, it got the very worst.

Crippling humidity, a floor that could swallow you whole at each step, and a population ready to feed on anyone who happened to end up there.

As I was treading with care on a log that lay between two dry patches of land, imagine my surprise when I felt that log twist around beneath my feet and reveal an ungodly amount of teeth on a pair of jaws closing in on me.

I jumped away, and fell chest deep in a slimy hole.

Because of the entangled heap of branches that surrounded me in the mud, swimming away wasn't an option.

Besides, the animal was better suited than me to move around in such an environment. I found an actual log, and managed to pull myself on it. With its two eyes on the top of its head, the alligator scanned its surroundings to find me, and it didn't take him long to locate me.

I went through my pockets for my knife, but couldn't find it. It had probably fallen during one of my horse riding stunts.

As I could feel the first bite coming, my fingers found something hard and potentially harmful in my coat.

I pulled it out. It was the phial Wilbur had sold me on credit. For a second, I thought of swallowing the contents, in the hopes of getting a quick and clean death. A very sad lesser of two evils, but I was pretty low on the hierarchy of beggars.

However, in a last act of despair, I threw it in the monster's gaping jaws.

It shattered, and for a moment, it perfectly assumed the role of an amuse bouche. The predator chewed on it angrily, giving me a preview of what was to happen to me.

I took advantage of the distraction to stand up on the log in the hopes of hiking up a tree. I had no climbing skills whatsoever, and the layering of years and fat did not help in the least.

However, in their magnanimity, the gods gave me a tree full of vines and solid branches that even a toddler holding his bottle would have been able to climb on without hesitation.

I also know that these same gods have a peculiar sense of humor. Which is why, instead of just grabbing away at vines like a hungry man at a full English breakfast buffet, I took hold of *one*, made sure it was of the vegetal denomination, and rolled it around my forearm as I went up. I did this for safety reasons, in case I inevitably fell, but also because any other vine was bound to be a snake, most likely poisonous.

Behind me, the alligator was thrashing angrily. But as long as I was able to get out of his reach, I could plan my next move.

Things were going well. I was easily eight feet above the ground, and was nearing a nice fat branch on which I could take a seat, breathe, wait for the crocodile to get bored, perhaps even settle down and start a new life.

The branch was a little away from the trunk, and all ll I had to do was take a leap of faith.

My vine was tightly strapped to my right arm, both feet were firmly locked in respectable nooks. I was ready.

I reached out towards the branch with my left arm. It was indeed a branch, not an anaconda or some other tropical monster. A good, peaceful branch. To get to it, all I had to do was to let go of the hold my feet were on.

So I jumped.

As it turned out, it was actually another tree. Which in itself, wasn't such a bad thing. All things considered, it wasn't another creature out to kill me.

However, that tree was leaning dangerously at an odd angle because it had been slowly crashing down for years. Its fall had been temporarily stopped by a nearby vine, making it look like an innocent branch. And since my body outweighed the upward pull of the vine, it allowed the tree to continue its journey downwards. With me tagging along.

But *aha*, I thought, I was prepared for such an eventuality: my right hand was still firmly attached to my safety vine. Unfortunately, the vine wasn't as firmly attached to the tree.

Somewhere above, something broke, and I fell all the way down, within the alligator's danger zone. And this time, I was neatly and entirely tied up in my safety vine.

I had become low-hanging fruit, ripe for the taking.

Which brings us back to the aforementioned peculiar sense of humor of the gods.

All I could wish was for the beast to go for a vital organ first, in order to make things quick, instead of slow and painful.

I closed my eyes, and just waited.

And waited.

I felt that the second I sneaked a peek was when it would decide to pounce on me, jaws wide open. So I chose to peek with one eye.

The giant lizard hadn't gone away. It was still there, in all its monstruous glory, a creature escaped from the realm of nightmares, designed to terrorize and rip apart.

Only something was slightly off.

It lay on its back, mouth gaping. One paw was twitching, but barely.

I pulled myself up with the help of my feet, and started untying my arm. My eyes were still on the croc. It wasn't its usual bloodthirsty self, but it didn't mean it would last. Especially that the twitching was gaining in momentum.

During my freefall, the vine had managed to tie a perfectly decent knot around my arm that would have made a sailor proud. I clawed at it with rising panic.

The reptile grunted, and seemed to be trying to shake off the daze it had been in.

"*Oh come on, that would be too stupid!*" I shouted.

Within a few seconds, I decided it best to cut my losses, and climb back up the tree. I planted my foot firmly in its hold, then pulled on the vine with everything I had...

…Only to remember it was no longer attached to the tree. I just stood there in front of the alligator. It brayed, and in a tremendous effort, turned on its stomach.

It buried its claws in the ground, and seemed to get re-acquainted with the world, reality, and the nagging awareness of a nearby lunch.

It was time to see if I could outrun a crocodile in a swamp.

Chapter 19

"Shave his belly with a rusty razor"

It is impressive how fast four little pudgy legs can go. They're not stubs, granted, they have joints and claws, but still. When you look at a horse's anatomy, you immediately understand it was born to run. A spider with its eight legs couldn't possibly be slow.

But the first person who ever laid eyes on one of these over-sized reptiles surely didn't imagine these buggers could be such hasty little devils.

That person probably didn't go on to have a nice day.

On the up side, the croc took a while to steady itself and come to terms with how edible I was, which gave me a bit of a running start. Nevertheless, it promptly made up for its delay.

In the water, it swam like a dolphin. On the mud, it darted as if on solid ground. And on solid ground, well, it went even faster. Especially that it didn't have to crouch under the branches and the annoying vegetation that got in my way. Where I had to do zigzags and gymnastics, it just plowed through.

By some sort of miracle, I made it back to an actual proper path, on which humans could run the way that allowed them to survive for so long.

So I ran, without looking back.

My plan was to get into town, where the locals probably had a protocol in case of an alligator attack. Even if it just meant putting a solid door between you and it, until it lost interest and waddled away.

My clothes had taken a serious toll from running carelessly through the jungle, but the fact that I was followed by a far more pressing distraction loosened up my pride. I was expecting everyone's stares to go from me to what ran after me.

As I barged in, I got the expected surprised looks. However, all eyes stayed on me.

As it turns out, crocodiles aren't comfortable away from their habitat, and aren't known to travel far just for a meal. I may have seemed interesting at first, but just not "throw-caution-to-the-wind" interesting.

Which left me as the main attraction in a populated part of town.

"Hey, you're that Gates person, aren't ya?" said a child holding a fishing pole. "Heard you had a bit too much of the old rum, didn't ya?"

"Here's our new police force!" said a woman with a loud voice. "Emilio says they're called the New CRAP!"

The roaring laughter made me almost miss mister Croc.

But at least, I was alive. Struck by a philosophical inspiration, I chose ridicule over death.

I proceeded towards Drake's Wreck, this time through town, where the environment was somehow less corrosive than the jungle.

~

This little adventure having seriously set me back way behind schedule, I darted down Shark Alley like a madman (clothes and accessories included), and ended up exhausted on Rock Beach. The wind had started to rise, and many of the stepping stones that led to the wreck were covered by the waves.

"This better be good," I said, imagining the wrath I'd unleash upon Nathaniel if it wasn't.

I was more than a little proud to see I remembered the stones pretty well. I could almost locate the entire path.

As any teacher would tell you, there's nothing worse than the confidence you get on your second try. You *think* you know enough, when you actually know diddly squat.

I didn't slip. To slip, I would have had to step on the rock first. What happened is that I missed it completely, and just sank.

It was very dark down there. At one point, I think I saw the shape of the sunken part of the wreck, and it terrorized me to my very soul. It looked disproportionately big, like an angry behemoth about to crush me under its belly. I felt I could sink forever, lost in that hateful void.

I swam back up, and finally got some fresh air. I was right next to the final rock. I climbed on it.

A gust of wind made my wet clothes ice cold, and a ripped sleeve slapped me across the face. Which goes to show that nothing good comes out of delaying bedtime. Nothing.

With one last hesitant hop, I landed on the main reef and ran to the ship.

"Nate, you still around?" I panted to the dark. "Apologies, getting here was everything but easy, but on the bright side, I didn't end up as a..."

I grew quiet. My words were echoing on empty walls. I could feel that no one was listening to me.

My eyes grew accustomed to the cool darkness, and I looked around for traces of him. It could have been something as subtle as a hair, or as obvious as his unconscious blood-covered body.

After nosing around, I got my reward. It had nothing to do with Nathaniel, but it was a new element for the investigation.

There were dark spots on the floor. At first, I dismissed them. Coming from a wet place, I was the cause of many of these spots. But something was bothering me. My dark spots were still fresh and wet, but there was another set that was just plain dark.

I crouched next to the biggest one, and ran my fingers over it. It was dry, so it was definitely not me. I compared it with the little puddle I had seen the previous day, and their hues seemed to match. Which meant that probably, Quickbit's body had been there first, where he lost the most blood. Had even probably been knocked out there.

So Redmayne struck him, but then he was moved to where he hung.

I looked around with a sense of urgency, seeing how fast the weather was darkening. I made a mental note to invest in matches as soon as I made it out of this mess.

There was rope lying everywhere, and it seemed sturdy enough to do the job of holding poor Quickbit up there.

Groping around to make up for my failing eyesight, I found a rope with a sharp end: this one had been cut recently.

I held it up next to the porthole to confirm what my fingers told me, and saw something. At first, I thought it was a play of shadows. The waves were getting excited in the background, and did funny things with the luminosity.

But on closer inspection, I saw little dots on the rope, where it had been cut. Dark little dots. Some fell off when I touched them. They reminded me of dried blood.

As I was looking through the porthole, I felt something was missing. An element had been taken away from the scene, but I couldn't put my finger on it.

Then, for just a split second, the whole world was saturated with light. Lightning struck, allowing me to see the sea, the shore, and the masts hanging up from Redmayne's shipyard. I saw her boat hooked up near her shack.

And that's when I remembered.

When we came with Nathaniel for the first time, there were two boats floating on the other side of the wreck. The abandoned tourist boats. But as I looked out, one was missing.

And that one, I realized, had been Redmayne's, the one she had rescued us in. Neither I nor Nathaniel had recognized it back then. I could have kicked myself.

She had been there, probably hiding, when we found the body.

I stepped out to a full-blown storm, not unlike the one that had greeted me. Only meaner.

"Good thing I'm not on a boat," I said to myself.

The stones that led back to the beach were now completely invisible, but the unease of staying near that wreck gave me the confidence to find them.

The first one was barely a few centimeters underneath the surf. With a steady enough footwork, I could get to shore safely.

Soaking wet, but on solid ground.

I eyed the stone, assessed my balance, looked up, and then froze. On the beach, right where I was supposed to land, stood a figure. A dark, hooded figure. With well-groomed curls.

~

She looked ominous.

To be fair, anyone dressed in black, standing still in stormy weather, with waves crashing at their feet, is bound to give out signals that generally mean: do not come near.

Part of my brain suggested that this person probably meant no harm, and was just taking an innocent stroll on the beach. But another part made the excellent point that, had that person been filled with only good intentions, she would have made it known by then. She could have waved, for instance. You know, the nice, decent, non-murderer thing to do.

You don't just look at someone about to walk on a life-threatening path without saying a word. The least you can do is give out some form of encouragement.

But no. She just stood there, waiting to see what would happen. And my instincts didn't like that. Not one bit.

I was soaked. Rain and seawater ran down my back, and I felt miserable.

"Hello?" I tried, in case she was just shy.

She did not even move. Her face was hidden, but I could feel her cold stare from under the hood.

Going back to shore was no longer an option. I had the low ground, low *and* slippery, and everybody knows that cannot end well.

I turned, and went back into the wreck.

The atmosphere there wasn't exactly feisty either. I was suddenly very aware that a dead body had been around not so long ago, and that some of his blood was smeared a bit everywhere.

Shadows started looking like silhouettes of Quickbit, sitting here, standing there, staring at me with his dead, empty sockets.

And while my imagination was having fun with me, my stalker was probably making her way to the wreck.

I could sense her appearing at the door every time I turned my back to it.

A new question popped in my head. If Redmayne had been there right before us, where had she been hiding while Nathaniel and I were sniffing around?

I looked at the porthole, and got my answer. She had escaped that way, which meant that I could do the same. And that was probably my best bet if I wanted to survive.

Of course, there was a part of me that wanted to wait for the mystery lady from the shore and confront her. Being the one to be on solid ground would have given me the advantage, and more importantly, made me look less like a coward.

But that would have been my *only* advantage.

I hadn't slept, I had just escaped a hungry reptile, and was in no shape to fight anyone, let alone fight a killer.

Run away and live to run another day.

I crawled out of the porthole. It wasn't exactly a gracious retreat, but the cold rain and the menacing waves made me feel better than the inside of the dead frigate.

And outside, I could see.

I walked to the edge of the ship, and peeked around the corner. The shape was no longer on the shore.

Either she had given up, or she was much closer. There was an easy way to know, but it led to a direct clash. Twenty years earlier, I would have been out there, sword and pistol drawn, ready to inflict some serious damage. But I no longer had it in me.

I heard a thump coming from the inside, and jumped.

She was there all right.

I looked at the stepping stones, and thought of making a run for it. But then what? She could just chase me, and if I didn't slip in the water to be carried away by some freak undertow, she would eventually catch up to me in the streets.

By now, she had probably come to the conclusion I was no longer inside. Thankfully, I had found a way out.

The little boat for tourists didn't look like much, but it floated, and it would keep on floating even if it capsized.

I made a run for it. At any point, a hand would grab me, and it would be over.

Instead of undoing the knot, I slipped it off the dock post, and jumped in the boat. My weight gave it enough momentum to start sailing away, and the waves did the rest.

Chapter 20

Constable at Sea

They say that once you are used to rowing, you never forget it.

To them I say: yes you do.

Picking up the oars and screwing them in the rowlocks came back naturally, I'll admit it. It even gave me a well-needed confidence boost.

But when the blades hit the waves, my illusion of mastery was blown to smithereens. The sea clearly did not intend to be tamed, and my grip was no match to its will. One of the oars was actually pried out of my fingers, and I caught it right before it slid into the water.

Instead of rowing, I had to settle for simply steering that rotten tub of a vessel away from the open sea. I knew I would eventually crash on the rocks scattered around the harbor's entrance, but it meant less chances of drowning.

Then another pesky complication came up.

The storm had only started half an hour ago, and the lighthouse guardian probably hadn't had the time to turn on his workplace. Seeing how New Cayenne had little to no sea traffic, it did not come as a surprise. He had probably stopped doing it altogether quite a while ago.

It did however make my life considerably more difficult, as I struggled to make sure the boat was headed in the proper direction. The clouds had grown thicker, and visibility was getting worse with each gust of wind.

Out of nowhere, stars appeared, but something was wrong; we were nowhere near the afternoon. Then my mind caught up.

The town had lights. If the lighthouse wasn't deemed as necessary, the inhabitants still needed to see through this unusual midday darkness. I could finally tell the difference between the shore and certain death.

Although, not quite.

There were also fishermen who had their lights on to attract the fish. I was no longer sure of which direction I was headed.

The hindsight part of my brain, which was starting to sound like Nathaniel, told me I should have stayed on solid ground, and faced the killer. And I actually agreed. A human taking on another human has approximately a fifty percent chance of making it.

A man taking on the ocean, on the other hand...

The water level inside the boat had been rising slowly but surely, despite my best efforts to ignore it. I would probably have to capsize it if I did not want it to sink.

Then, out of the darkness where I was headed, something darker emerged. I immediately thought of Saul and his kraken.

It rose at a whooping hundred feet, and I would have taken it for a sea monster of the apocalypse had I not made out the masts.

I could not remember seeing such a ship when I arrived, which made me fear for how far I had gone adrift.

Going towards it was entirely out of the question. I would crash on the hull before anyone would notice, let alone hear me screaming in this storm.

So I rowed.

The old reflexes kicked in, and I finally got a grip of the waves. I steered away from it.

"Come on, you poor excuse of a boat, do not fail me," I prayed out loud.

It apparently got offended, and chose to fail me.

The pressure between my grip and the current was too great. One of the oars snapped like a twig, and I was hurled once again towards the monster.

"Oh, all right Nathaniel, you were right!" I screamed at the raging wind. "I should have listened to you, you were right all along, and I have just been making one bad choice after another! Happy? I'll have this carved on my tombstone if I ever get a grave! Although I'll probably end up in the belly of a fish. Hope it makes you laugh, Nate! Hope I end up on your plate, and that you choke on one of my fish bones!"

I crashed into the ship.

My boat shattered as if it were made of sticks. Not only were the remaining pieces useless, but they were quickly scattered away, leaving me to drown like the idiot that I was.

I held my breath, and failed.

Drowning is one of the most unpleasant ways to go. The water in your lungs is unbearable, you suffocate, and the little air you manage to get in is useless. Your heart panics, pounds in your chest, in your throat, in your ears. You try to coordinate your movements, but the waves slow you down, they bully you into submission.

And drowning under the keel of a fairly large ship is even worse. You feel like a little piece of nothing crushed under the belly of an angry sea monster. Zero redeeming qualities.

My legacy on this island would turn out to be a cautionary tale. The inhabitants would use expressions along the lines of "unlucky like a policeman among pirates".

Then a tentacle hit me.

I would have screamed "*certainly you can't be serious,*" if it hadn't meant swallowing a deadly amount of seawater.

Instead, I chose to fight back. Whatever sea creature had deemed it funny to kick me when I was already down was eating me with one tentacle less.

I bit it with everything I had. And by God, did it feel good. Violence may be the worst solution, but something has to be said about its short-term cathartic benefits. I immediately felt better, and empowered.

Better yet, the tentacle didn't pull me down, and for a very good reason: it wasn't a tentacle. It was harder, almost stiff, and covered with a pattern that made me think of braids.

I pulled on it and confirmed that it was in fact a rope. A rope that seemed to be attached to the ship.

In spite of the warring waves and waterspouts, I climbed up against the hull. Every step forward was followed by ten steps backwards. With that kind of math, I wasn't going anywhere.

But then, the rope started pulling *me* instead.

The chances of it being divine Providence were close to none. If I was being pulled out of the frying pan, it was to be thrown right into the fire. Someone on this ship was behind it, and would probably not be thrilled to see me as the catch of the day.

I had to find a place to hold on to right before the deck.

However, visibility was so bad I had no way of knowing where the deck was, or where I could latch on to.

Out of the darkness, somewhere behind the howling of the storm, I heard a voice. At first, it was very faint, to the point where I had to almost use my imagination to hear it. But as I went up, it became clearer.

Someone was groaning, probably because of my weight. It was not a nice groan either. It sounded mean, coarse, and cruel. This was definitely not the welcoming committee.

It was when I could almost smell the alcohol on the puller's breath that I chose to leap. It was a big ship, I was bound to find something to hang on to.

But it was too late.

I felt the deck under my feet, and had to jump above the railing.

"What's going on?" shouted a voice.

"I'm fixing your mistakes, that's what's going on!" answered a voice right in front of me.

I crouched, and rolled to my left.

"Bring the light, will you? I think something got stuck to the rope."

"You know we're not supposed to use lights outside."

"Yes, but this rope wasn't supposed to be let down at sea, *bring a light!*"

Squatting, I groped for a mast or a barrel for me to hide behind.

There was a flash of light.

I was halfway behind a crate, and quickly rolled myself into a ball.

"See? Nothing."

"Wait! Don't turn it off, I swear there was something holding on to the rope."

"You've just grown weak. Or it was probably stuck to a hatch or something, like that stupid net we caught the other day."

"At least that thing had been full of fish."

"Maybe that was another, and you just dropped it with your clumsy paws."

Another groan.

"Fine, turn the light off."

Everything was dark gray again.

"Shouldn't she be here by now?"

"Everything should be over by now, if you ask me. Had *we* been on the ground, everything would have been properly done."

"I heard the ones you tried to kill made it."

"What are you talking about?"

"The ones meant to drown in the cove."

"Them? They were supposed to live. It was a plan or something. Waste of time, again."

"So, what do we do?"

"If she's not on board by tomorrow, I say we leave."

"I meant now."

"Now we go back in."

Still crouching, I tried to follow their voices. I needed to know who "she" was.

Of course that was the moment that something had to get in my way. I can't exactly say what it was, but there were wooden sticks, strings, metallic joints, and it went *clang* a few times.

"Yes, I heard it this time," said one of the goons.

"Who's there?"

I picked up the mess I was entangled in. Luckily, only one leg was caught. If push came to shove, I could always hop to freedom.

"Very well!" shouted the first goon.

The crate that hid me exploded. It wasn't pushed or even cast away. It exploded. It contained bottles that fell everywhere, and all I could do was jump.

"The light, you idiot, the light!"

It came on at the moment I performed my award-winning angel's leap.

Had they seen me? Had they recognized me? Would I survive my daring escape? And most importantly, did I look good doing it?

I crashed in the waves. I tried swimming away, but the current kept pushing me back to the ship.

A new emotion took over, a stronger one: anger.

I hated myself, I hated the whole world for not letting me solve this case, which felt somehow worse than being eaten by a dark and cold ocean. Especially that I was so close to solving it.

I chose to go down fighting.

I kicked myself away with both feet before being entirely swallowed under the ship and tried to dog paddle my way out of it. Almost instantly, I was hurled back on the unforgiving keel.

I remembered Nathaniel's little story about these people from Mina and their peculiar way of swimming. I tried to follow what I remembered of his instructions. It was at best a very loose interpretation.

But it worked.

After a few strokes, I looked over my shoulder. I had distanced myself from the Man O'War. Not that I was entirely sure, since everything was blurred in darkening shades of black, but its oppressive presence didn't feel as close.

I continued moving away from the ship, hoping to be headed towards the shore. At the very least, I was going somewhere that didn't spell immediate death.

A wave went over my head, and all of a sudden, I could not move. Something grabbed my hands and feet. It was too solid for seaweed. I tried to tear it apart, and realized it was actually an army of well organized strings. The strings from the complicated thing that had hung on to me. A fishing net, attached to a wooden device. I was not going to make it after all.

Maybe it was better that way. This whole affair had been off to a terrible start, everyone wanted me dead, and I wasn't sure I wanted me alive either. A fisherman would eventually find me, and if he wasn't too strung up on work ethics, would temporarily add red meat on his display.

Then, something pulled me away with superhuman strength. There were also creatures underwater that didn't wish me well. I had escaped a crocodile, but that didn't mean I couldn't be eaten by a shark.

Curiously enough, though, the shark pulled me out of the water, and threw me on a solid, wooden floor.

I turned face down, and threw up half the ocean on my savior's boat.

"You may just be the oddest catch I ever made, and that's saying something," said a familiar voice.

Chapter 21

A Big Fish Story

I looked around in disbelief.

Under the light of a swinging storm lantern, I recognized Wilbur's crazed face. He had the look of a man who lived comfortably in that stretch between sanity and full-on bonkers. His hair dancing wildly in the wind didn't help.

"Thank you," I finally managed.

"How did you end up here?"

"Oh, it's a long and stupid story."

"It's precisely that kind of story that makes the world go round."

I looked at his scrawny arms maneuvering the sails of his schooner, and remembered how he had effortlessly plucked me out of the sea.

"You're freakishly strong, do you know that?"

"A healthy diet and proper self-care (with the right products) can go a long way."

I remembered his potion and what it did to the alligator.

The deadly potion that had been intended for me.

I realized he had probably not known who he was saving, or else he would have left me to drown.

I suddenly felt very vulnerable lying down in the ship of a man who had planned on poisoning me. And because standing up wasn't the safest position on a rocking boat either, I opted for a defensive crouch.

"And how come *you* are out in such a horrible weather?" I asked him.

"Fish caught during a storm have very strong healing properties. Makes you smarter. Calmer. Good for gonorrhea. And so much more."

I looked at him with fresh eyes. I had completely neglected to consider him as a suspect. Rookie mistake. Everyone's a suspect, always. It's true that the man did not profit from killing people, but making them sick suited him perfectly. He needed an unwell customer base. Or a scared one.

"Now that I've answered your question, will you be answering mine?" he insisted.

"I was chased here by the killer."

"Oh, I see."

His face remained as relaxed as a freshly tanned hide in the sun. Not a twitch, not a tell. Maybe he already knew. Maybe he had gone out to sea in order to find me and tie the last loose end.

"Mind if I bother you with a few questions?" I asked.

"Ah, no matter how dire the situation is, your job always comes first. We are both very much alike."

"Yes, I'm sure I agree, on some level."

"I know you see me as a charlatan, Gates. Even my most loyal customers do. But they still come back to me because I give them something no one else does."

"One-size-cures-all potions?"

"I give them hope in miracles. Hope in the impossible. And it's sometimes *that one ingredient* that makes the difference, that'll give them the extra push to fight just a bit more."

"I guess I can't argue with that... But I apologize, my intention was not to insult you, especially not after saving my life."

And especially not when I find myself at your mercy.

He laughed.

"Don't worry, I have no pride outside of my successes. Everything else is just sticks and stones, Gates, sticks and stones."

Why was he keeping me alive? To give me the big reveal before throwing me overboard?

"What was your actual relationship with Solomon Quickbit?"

"My *actual* relationship? Did I ever have one that was... Not actual?"

He was trying to know what I knew, to see if I was really worth killing.

"I know everyone hated him," I said. "And that almost no one batted an eyelid when he died. Quite sad, if you ask me."

Wilbur pulled on the sail and veered towards a wave that would have done some serious damage had it hit us sideways.

"The more you betray people, the smaller the crowd at your funeral," he finally stated.

"Indeed. So he betrayed you?"

"He paid on time. Always."

"A regular?"

"You could say that. Solomon had demons that terrorized him, and he needed something to help him sleep."

"A good and loyal customer then. You must have been one of the few, if not the only one, to have been displeased with his passing."

"I never rejoice in the death of a fellow human being."

"So it must hurt even more knowing he died with arsenic in his system."

He smirked.

"Once one of my products has left the ship, it is no longer my responsibility."

"Even if it also killed Admiral Winchester?"

"Would you arrest a swords merchant?"

"One could argue that swords are meant for defense as well. Arsenic is exclusively for killing."

"Every poison can be a cure, depending on the dosage."

"Oh, and were you planning on telling me that at *my* funeral?"

For the first time, he looked genuinely confused.

"Unless I misunderstood," I continued, "and that was just some sort of morbid practical joke."

"Forgive me, but I have no idea what you're hinting at."

"*Your Bad Juju Away potion!*" I shouted.

"I understand it is a bit on the sour side, but I assure you it goes down better with milk, or rum, or even both with some honey..."

"Thankfully I wasn't the one to ingest it."

"You... Tested it on someone else?"

"Why, was that dangerous?"

"No, but since you seem to think it is, it comes out as a bit devious, don't you think?"

"I fed it to a crocodile that was trying to eat me!"

"A crocodile... Caiman?"

"I'm sorry, the subject didn't pop up during our conversation."

"East of the town limits? Next to the graveyard?"

This interrogation was not going as expected.

"Yes, I suppose."

"You met Steve! How did it go?"

"Thankfully not the way it usually goes when one meets a crocodile."

"Caiman."

"Oh whatever!"

"You fed him the content of my phial?"

"To be honest, I gave him the whole package, potion, phial and all. Not the way you intended it, but I felt it increased the chances of keeping the full count of my fingers."

"No worries there I'm sure, Steve's not a picky eater."

"You don't say."

"He's eaten worse, without even making a fuss."

"Funny you should say that, because it actually sent him into a slight coma."

He blinked.

"That's impossible."

"Do you deny giving me poison?" I asked point blank, tired of beating around the bush.

"Wholeheartedly! I just saved you, didn't I?"

"So you're saying you gave me poison by mistake?"

"No, and there were no mistakes. And arsenic won't kill a caiman, not even harm it. Especially not in that quantity. Unless..."

He pulled out the fishnet, and emptied it next to me. I had to move away from half a dozen slimy flapping fish.

"You know," he smiled, "it's funny, but what I gave you contains a serum that, if mixed with arsenic, can be a strong soporific for reptiles. You didn't by any chance throw in some arsenic as well?"

"No, just the phial you gave me."

"Hmm. That's very odd. You say he dozed off?"

"Well, one second he was chasing me up a tree, and the next, he was lying on the side."

"And how long did it last?"
"A few minutes, tops?"
"Definitely arsenic and my formula."
"Have you used it a lot?"
"More than a few times, yes, when looking for rare herbs in the island's swamps. Had to find a way to peacefully neutralize some predators, since I'm not keen on killing, in spite of what you think. Especially not Steve."
Without a warning, he jumped out of the boat. I ran to the helm, bracing myself for having to pull him back from the waves, and saw him on the dock, tying the ship to a bollard.
"Oh we're back?"
"I sure hope so, or else we're both hallucinating and I'm dead. I take it you enjoyed the trip?"
"It's so dark, I didn't notice us entering the harbor."
"It's also hard to notice things when you're crouching. Reassured I won't throw you out now?"
I climbed out, trying not to look as ashamed as I felt.
"Apologies, Wilbur. But it's been a trying day, and I feel everyone is after me."
"I've got just the potion for this."
"Let me first pay you for the previous one. And I might need more if I ever run back into Steve."
"So, what is your next move, mister policeman?"
"Find out who tried to kill me. And see if Nathaniel's still alive."
There was one place where I could find answers.

Chapter 22

The Shark's Lair

Where would Nathaniel want to go? Probably to the most dangerous place on the island. Quickbit and Redmayne had to disappear for being annoying witnesses. And the person who turned them against each other was the one who had poisoned Winchester. So who was it?

At the Admiral's manor, security was as tight as the choking grip of a desperate man. The heavily funded militia hired by the Lilac Hill homeowner association was everywhere.

I would have to sneak in like a thief.

From our drunken escape, I had remembered seeing a tree whose branches went over the property walls.

What I couldn't have known was that on the other side of that wall, where the branches reached out, was a steep cliff that ended on sharp rocks. As I looked down, I even thought I could make out the bony remains of an unlucky person.

All around the estate, the walls were high and perfectly polished. There wasn't the slightest nook in which one could get a decent foothold.

The only climbable part was precisely that area above the deadly cliff. It had been neglected by the preservation team for two probable reasons. First of all, no salary can justify risking your life for the sake of a stupid wall. And second, the absence of floor in front of it was a dissuasive enough point against any potential intruder. But mostly the first reason.

And thus, it offered a whole spectrum of irregularities that would have made the joy of any seasoned mountaineer. I chose not to let the fact that I wasn't a seasoned mountaineer get in the way.

The skies had finally cleared up, and the sunset light enhanced the shapes of these irregularities, making them all the more accessible.

I tried my luck at the very edge of the cliff, and discovered it wasn't as hard as expected. The sun's fading warmth had dried the rain on the wall, making every bump and crack rough enough for my feet to take hold.

I went for it.

It quickly became a game. Every time I found a proper foothold, I instantly started looking for the next one. I enjoyed getting the hang of it, pun shamelessly intended, and almost saw why some did it for pleasure. Even my fingers, who always had a hard time dealing with everyday tasks, seemed enthusiastic.

I got lost in the moment.

All it took was a quick glance to my left.

The ledge was no longer within reach. I didn't have to look down to know I was hanging right above the chasm, far, far away from what I thought of as my safety net.

At that very moment, the little muscles in my fingers didn't want to play anymore. My grip was slowly weakening.

I looked up towards the branch. I wasn't there yet. I was no longer able to find proper holds, my momentum had dwindled to a full stop.

"It's all going to be perfectly fine..." I said to the wall.

My right foot slipped, but my three other extremities were solidly secured.

"Not today, you treacherous... Hole in the wall."

I found a better hold in the crack between two bricks, and hauled myself up.

I thought of the skeleton down below. Who was it? Why had they decided to try their luck there? And what part of the climbing went wrong for them to end up like that?

I had the feeling that I may just get some unwanted answers.

I reached up, and felt the branch with the tip of my fingers. By stretching myself to the limit, I could almost grab it.

~

It came at the right moment, since the wall at that point had become smooth again. Probably because that part was easier to fix from up there.

Moving up a few extra inches, I took hold of the branch, and gave it a tug.

It felt solid.

I knew it was not in my best interest to put my entire hopes on that single branch, but it was perfect to give me the boost I needed to reach the top of the wall. Afterwards, I would only have to set my panic free, and fling myself over to the other side.

The idea of falling on the lawn inside was almost comforting, compared to the cliff underneath.

"There goes nothing..."

I actually let go, and put all my weight on the branch, expecting it to let out a loud crack.

But it stayed whole.

I grabbed it with both hands, and went all in. If I was to know what had happened to the poor bloke down there, that was the moment.

I pulled myself up, and to my surprise, I made it all the way to my chest. No ominous breaking sound, no surprise bend, just a sturdy branch like I used to climb on as a child.

The rest of my body followed smoothly. I even felt I could just haul myself inside the tree, so I did just that.

I found myself at the perfect vantage point. I could see the whole estate, the guards moving back and forth, the entrances, everything.

I quickly noticed that in the back, security wasn't as tight. It looked more like a facade kind of measure, since after all, the man they were supposed to protect no longer needed it. It's just that the neighbors had to see that his estate wasn't taking things lightly.

After all, his wife, the legal heir, was still missing.

In less time than it takes Nathaniel to come up with a dodgy joke, I had a plan. All I needed to do was to crawl in the bushes behind a group of guards. Since their gazes were focused on a neighboring window where some lady was getting dressed, I could safely make my way to the mansion, and enter the kitchen door.

Afterwards, I would have to improvise.

I felt something move over my head, and did what I should have done *before* entering the tree.

I looked around.

What the corner of my eyes had dismissed as regular Caribbean vines, turned out to be a slithering mess of snakes. Long, black snakes. They were everywhere, coiled around the branches, hanging down, crawling closer. The whole tree seemed to be made of snakes.

Besides a deep feeling of awe in the presence of such a phenomenon, I mostly wanted to scream. A nice, long, liberating scream, which would obviously have solved nothing, but would have allowed me to release the terror that had been building up in my poor nerves.

For a second, I even considered fainting. But since it would have sent me hurling down to a certain death, I decided not to. On a side note, it was probably what had happened to mister Bones down there.

I took a deep breath, crouched, and tried to calculate the best way to jump down on the other side of the wall, while doing my best to ignore my crawling companions.

One of the guards was saying something highly spiritual on what they were witnessing, which got everyone's attention back towards the garden.

I couldn't jump just yet.

But then one of the snakes helped me change my mind.

It crept up my leg, mistaking it probably for a branch, and squeezed itself around it. That was precisely where I drew the line in my relationship with reptiles.

I leaped in the garden, and started hopping on one leg in the direction of the kitchen door. I was perhaps losing my mind, but I wasn't letting that get in the way of my plan.

For a split second, it looked like no one would see me. The guards were still guffawing at their joke, not caring one bit about a jumping rag doll with a long black snake around its leg.

And I almost cuooooded, mind you.

The lady in the window had made a comeback, and the troop of voyeurs was ogling again, jaws slacking.

There was absolutely no need to sneak. I could have danced my way to the kitchen, which I technically did, without getting any attention.

The snake, though, did not care much for my frantic fidgeting. He made it clear to me by shoving his triangular head right into my crotch.

At that point, I had to scream. No way around it. *That* was the straw that finally broke the perverted group of camels' backs. Or ears.

I had the guards' full attention. And they didn't take long to decide to charge me at once.

Since panic had over-clouded my fears and inhibitions, I managed to grab the snake's head, and yank him out of his grip. I then proceeded to swing the poor reptile over my head like a sling, and throw it at them in a way that would have worried a certain biblical giant. I screamed again, in an attempt at a war cry. They screamed back, terrorized, and just scattered.

I ran inside.

~

I was greeted by quite a few surprised faces. It was apparently the time in the evening when everybody in the house had to be in the kitchen.

Of course there were the cooks and the expected servants. But I was surprised to see plenty of guards as well. Had I chosen to enter the house literally anywhere else, I could have casually strolled through the empty hallways unhindered.

I had planned on improvising. I chose to sprint.

Everyone was too stunned to do anything else but watch me run. One of them shouted "hey, you!" Another jumped out of my way. Nothing more.

I got to the Admiral's office in no time, panting but unscathed, and I think not even entirely identified.

Once in there, I turned the key in the lock as many times as possible, grabbed Winchester's big office chair, and shoved it against the door, right under the handle.

I went behind the desk, and looked around. I had to search as thoroughly as possible, hoping to find something I had missed.

The paperwork was as we had left it. Uninteresting financial affairs, letters on the state of his businesses, official papers, and a petition to make the tenants of Lilac Hill pay their share of the main wall's preservation.

His signature was missing.

"I guess I owe you that one, my dear Godefroy."

But under that paper, I saw a list of numbers with the name Jack Boots on top of it. Money. And what's more, money he owed. Redmayne wasn't the only one deep into debt.

I straightened myself up to look closer, and my foot struck something underneath the desk.

"Come out of there!" ordered a hesitant voice from the other side of the door.

"Yes, yes, in a minute."

The voice broke into a whisper, joined by many others.

"Don't force that door open, you don't want to damage it, it would lower the manor's resale value!" one of the whisperers whispered a bit too loud.

Angry whispered replies told him *I* didn't need to know that.

I bent down, and picked up what had been hidden under the chair.

It was a glass, with some reddish sediments in it. It smelled of wine. And something sour.

"Gates, that you?" said a familiar voice.

"Mister Sneer, so good to hear you!" I said.

"I advise you not to do anything stupid," he warned.

"Oh, I'm afraid I'm way beyond stupid at this point. But don't worry, I'm almost done here."

"What in the nine circles of hell do you think *you're* doing?" asked a voice inside the room.

I turned around with a startle, and saw a woman.

She wore a dark crimson leather coat. Her long auburn hair was kept undone under a top hat that matched the coat. She also held a rapier.

Incidentally, its pointy end was a few inches from my chest.

I jumped back, which caused me to sit clumsily on the desk.

"Hello there! Lady Winchester, I presume?"

She moved forward.

"Answer me!" she hissed.

"Well first of all, my sincerest condolences for your-"

She lunged, but I had been expecting it. I did an elegant spin on the desk, of which I am very proud of to this day, and found myself on the other side.

"It does not have to happen this way, milady."

"Oh but I think it does."

She moved fast. What she wore was meant to facilitate moving on a stage, and incidentally, in a duel.

In a stride or two, she was once again on my side of the desk, her back to the door.

"Give me one good reason as to why I shouldn't kill you this instant," she said, ready to strike.

"Well, for starters, because it doesn't look good to kill a copper. Usually works against you in front of a jury."

"The police? Among pirates?"

"Still a work in progress, but it could be promising, as long as you don't kill me."

"What brings you to nose around my late husband's affairs?"

"It's funny, *he* was the one to come to me, and it was because of you."

"But now he's dead, and Mister Christopher and all the staff seem to think you're the culprit."

"Mister Christopher… Oh yes, Sneer."

"Sneer?"

"Doesn't he look like a Sneer to you? With the expression he has on his face…"

"*Mister Gates,*" Sneer brayed in a sing-song voice, "*you have five seconds to open this door, or you'll come to regret it!*"

Outside, there was a full-blown board meeting about the importance of keeping the integrity of the house intact, and even Sneer wasn't able to steer the opinion in his direction.

"If it wasn't you," Lady Winchester said, "then who was it?"

"With the whole population dropping like flies, the number of suspects grows smaller."

She narrowed her eyes.

"You suspect *me*."

"For what it's worth, I suspect everyone, including the victim when she happens to have survived."

"Is this the best you can do to convince me to spare your life? That you think I killed my husband?"

"Yes, I heard it now, and it doesn't sound so good."

I wasn't used to having suspects being so aggressive towards officers of the law. Typical down-to-earth land people soiled their breeches whenever an agent so much as looked at them funny. People used to bend over backwards to make me believe they were innocent.

But here? I was nothing more than an annoyance. Killing me wouldn't have been seen as an admission of guilt, but as an entirely acceptable (if not celebrated) outcome.

"I'm sure you have a lot to say in your defense," I risked.

She lifted an eyebrow.

"No wait, I can do better!"

I most certainly didn't believe I could. I cleared my throat, and remembered to keep my voice as low as possible.

"You were drawn into this against your own will. A lot of people are against you, and you had to react."

"Speak louder, we can't hear a word!" said a voice from the waiting room.

"You see, now *that's* whispering," said another.

"Gates, who are you talking with?" asked Sneer.

Lady Winchester looked at me like a tiger about to pounce.

"Go on," she said.

I hesitated, surprised to having made it this far.

"Redmayne was not planning on reimbursing your husband, and Quickbit had stolen from you as well. And he was blackmailing you. One of them killed your husband, and you defended yourself by getting rid of both. Fair and square. Any jury would forgive you for this! Especially a jury made of pirates."

"I could almost trust you if you weren't working for the mayor."

Things were starting to make sense.

"Right, *he* owes you money as well. That's why you wanted to kill him too."

"You are excruciatingly bad at this. The others can have your corpse once I am done with you."

She swung her sword.

When handled with skill, a good blade doesn't need much force to cut through a throat like a knife in warm butter. It's all in the wrist, really. And Kathy Winchester was tremendously skilled. I saw it in the ease with which she casually aimed for my neck.

Too bad her timing was off by a few seconds.

With a big slam, the doors opened. The people on the other side had finally decided to accept Sneer's suggestion of brute force.

The corner of one door caught her on the temple, bludgeoning her into oblivion.

"Do you think that dent was there before?" asked one of the servants.

"I *told* you to hit on the left side, you half-boiled potato!" answered another.

Sneer swooped in, and sneered at me. But this time, it looked like a triumphant smile.

"I knew it!"

"You did?" I asked, almost relieved.

"You two were in on it together!"

"You… Does your mind naturally go in the wrong direction, or did you need some special kind of training?"

"I knew," his voice quivered, "the second you set foot on this island, you were bad news, what with Lady Winchester disappearing and all. I feared for my master's life, I did! And I was right, wasn't I? Boys?"

The others were too preoccupied to assess the damage, and if any of it would have some incidence on their salary.

"Oh never mind... Guards, seize these no good murderers!"

"What right do *you* have to arrest me?"

"I am master of the estate, until further notice. And that'll teach you to call me 'Sneer'."

"It's just that it suits you so well."

Chapter 23

"Two men to man the wheel"

I finally managed to sleep.

When you're tired enough, any surface, no matter how rough and uncomfortable, can become a proper bed.

The jail wagon was starting to be a familiar place. I nodded at the driver, and went straight to the front right corner of the sweat box. For some reason, that spot got less hate from the road's accidental pavement.

I sprawled on the bench, crossed legs and arms, and closed my eyes. The guards carrying Lady Winchester said nothing. In their experience, someone displaying that level of confidence had a good card up their sleeve.

And in a way, I did.

The case was almost entirely solved, I just needed to try a few things at my trial. Not a sentence any lawyer would be thrilled to hear, I'll admit.

~

My arrival lacked panache.

Waking up was a bit tougher than expected. Napping had not been a good idea. I felt numb and comatose.

I was welcomed with a deafening silence. And stares, the kind you save for death row candidates.

The mayors, both present and future, were there. Boots was sitting behind his desk. Bartholomew, as usual, was standing behind him. Selena Montgomery was in her spot, and all traces of kindliness were gone from her face.

The only thing missing were pitchforks and torches.

"Gates," Boots finally said. "You had been hired to help fix the island's reputation as a lawless place."

"Mayor Boots, with all due respect, you should really..."

"You have absolutely *no* authority to speak! When Admiral Winchester's body turned up, I was willing to give you the benefit of the doubt. But 'accidentally' being the first one to discover a dead person has its limits. And now this? Breaking into a house? What kind of policeman acts this way?"

He had a point. Had I not been me, I would have been against me as well.

"I agree with the last part, but I had good reasons to..."

"I am not finished." His right hand was trembling. "What makes things worse, is that we have now proof that you had entered Admiral Winchester's room when he was killed, which cancels your first alibi. You lied from the start."

Two armed men walked in with Nathaniel, shackles on, his smartass grin completely gone.

By asking him to come to Town Hall, I had thrown him into a trap.

"This man, *your* assistant, was found with *this* book in his possession."

Boots held up a black leathery book I immediately recognized. Blackbeard's cookbook. A brief glimpse of Nate burning on it in a fiery inferno flashed in my mind. The idiot had stolen it back from Reine and Félix.

"Do you still deny entering the Admiral's office *before* mister Christopher went in?"

Lying was still an option. It always is. I was in pirate country, surrounded by people whose livelihood was based on lies and deceit.

But I was curious to see if I could talk myself out of this rut simply with the truth.

"No, I do not deny it."

Grunts and sniggers from the crowd. I think I even heard a "told you so". Bartholomew raised an eyebrow.

"So do you confess to the murders of Admiral Winchester," Boots asked, his voice building up to a crescendo, "Solomon Quickbit, and Captain Clarisse Redmayne, with the intent of destabilizing this town's fragile equilibrium? Were you sent by the Crown? Or any crown for that matter? Do you work with Woodes Rogers?"

Everybody spat on the floor at the mention of his name.

"That's a lot of questions, mister mayor, and I intend to answer each and every one of them. So, hold on," I started counting on my fingers, "no, no, no, no, and, if I am not mistaken, no. Hold on, that's one 'no' too many."

"Do not make a mockery of this trial, mister Gates," said Bartholomew.

"Funny you should call this improvised assembly a trial, Mister Bartholomew, I thought you were a lawyer."

"When caught red-handed," he replied, "one cannot pretend to have the moral high ground. It *is* a spontaneous and unorthodox trial, I grant you this, but considering the circumstances, it is a trial nonetheless."

"Well then, I should be able to plead my case, shouldn't I? In spite of all the damning evidence?"

Selena's eyes darted sideways when I looked at her. Someone had rigged the dice, but who?

"I take it you plead not guilty?"

"Something along those lines. I can even tell you what actually happened, with the name of the culprit and all."

"If you're planning on dumping it all on lady Winchester," Boots said, "I suggest you save your breath. She clearly did not act alone."

"I'd rather use my breath as much as possible before the noose puts an end to it, if it's all the same to you."

Mayor Boots looked at Bartholomew, who gave him a small nod.

"Very well, Gates. Speak."

"Why thank you."

I cracked my neck. Outside, I could hear the seagulls complaining about the weather that was once again turning sour.

"We did enter Admiral Winchester's office before he was officially found. However, he was already dead at the time."

"And why didn't you sound the alarm?"

"Because we knew we would be framed for it. It was perhaps not the best decision, since we are *still* being accused of this crime," I glared at Nathaniel, "but it gave us time to carry on with the investigation, before all the trails went cold. And this is what we learned."

I looked at the crowd surrounding me. Everybody listened.

"It was poison that killed Admiral Winchester."

That got me a reaction. A few gasps, nothing wild, but all it takes is a light breeze to overturn the weather.

"As it was poison that killed Solomon Quickbit, and Captain Redmayne."

"Don't mean to interrupt," interrupted Sneer, "but that blade through his chest didn't look much like poison to me."

He got a few laughs.

"The sword was planted there *after* he was poisoned. Before you ask me how I found this out, know that we had his body examined by Reine and Félix, which you all trust with your lives if I am not mistaken."

"And what tells us it wasn't *you* who gave him the poison before stabbing him?" asked Boots.

"It would indeed be plausible," I answered, "had the Admiral and I been on drinking terms. But as you are aware, such an amount of arsenic cannot be forced into someone, it has to be taken willingly. Winchester thought he was having an innocent glass of wine, just like Quickbit, and Redmayne. I knew that these two ingested the poison with wine, but I had to be sure about Winchester. Which is why I went back up to his office."

"So why sneak up there like a thief?" asked Boots. "Your acts are more those of a criminal wanting to erase his tracks, than those of an appointed representative of the law."

"Going there officially would have prompted the culprit to erase *their* tracks, precisely," I said, leering at Sneer.

"Do you have the nerve of accusing me?" he asked with an outrage that was almost comical.

"You were pretty quick to pin the murder on us, weren't you?" I cut back.

"You lying, scumbag of an outsider," he stammered, "what makes you think you can just waltz in here and start pointing your dirty little finger-"

"But sadly, you are not the culprit either. Trust me, it would have given me great pleasure. As it is, you are as guilty as you are sharp."

"Whu?"

"You're innocent, Mister Christopher, is what he's saying," explained Boots, visibly impatient.

"Oh," Sneer begrudgingly acknowledged.

"Well, maybe not *entirely* innocent as such, but you killed no one," I specified.

Sneer grimaced, sensing a trap, but deemed it wiser to just shut up and wait. He hadn't survived this long without a smidgeon of self-preservation.

"This is how it went. Our murderer, whom we'll call X..."

"Who's X?" asked someone in the crowd.

"The murderer," answered a man, who upon inspection turned out to be Saul.

"What kind of name is X?"

"It's meant to build suspense for the big reveal."

"Who is he calling fat?"

"He's making his story more interesting, you daft barnacle!" said Saul. "He says X, to keep you wondering, and in the end, he tells us who X is."

"He just said it's the killer. If anything, you're the daft one!"

I cleared my throat as if a whale had been caught in it. Everyone looked back at me, reluctant to abandon Saul and the barnacle's highly instructional exchange.

"May I go on?" I asked. "Good. So X owes Admiral Winchester money, but can't pay him back."

"So X kills the Admiral!" deduced the daft barnacle.

"Exactly! But in order not to get caught, X frames other people, like Quickbit, and Redmayne, who owe him money as well."

I looked around, to see if I had succeeded in going from suspect to showrunner. The looks I got were mixed, but encouraging. The rope wasn't around my neck just yet.

"But that was a tricky situation, because framed people tend to fight back. So X turned them against each other."

"Sneaky," said Saul, appreciative.

"Indeed, but it gets sneakier. X poisoned the two of them, so that the one who came out alive from the confrontation would end up dead as well."

"That X person is quite the mastermind," said the daft barnacle."

"And how did that *actually* play out?" asked Bartholomew, an inkling of impatience in his voice.

"Redmayne confronted Quickbit at Drake's End. Threats were exchanged. Swords were drawn. And inevitably, blood was spilled."

"Who won?" asked Saul.

"The poison got the best of Quickbit. But Redmayne thought she had dealt the mortal blow. So she hanged him, to cover her tracks."

I gave them time to visualize the scene, letting them add the gruesome details in their minds.

"That gave the real killer enough blackmail material for a while. However, something rushed her fate."

I felt that Selena and Nathaniel's demeanor had relaxed, but I decided to ignore it, knowing that too much optimism never led to anything good.

"My assistant and I followed her to a secret meeting with the culprit. In spite of our highly discreet stance, Redmayne's blackmailer saw us, and knew she had been compromised. She had to die."

"He *stabbed* her in cold blood," the barnacle said.

"*No*, you nitwit," scolded Saul. "She was poisoned, can't you ever listen properly like everyone else? Aren't I right mister Gates?"

"Indeed you are, my friend, indeed you are. By a poisoned bottle of wine, a wine that I almost drank from. Sadly, she drank it first, just to prove it was safe."

"If I understand correctly, mister Gates," said Bartholomew, "you convinced her to drink that wine before you."

"Again, a very good point, had captain Redmayne been a gullible enough person to accept wine from someone like me. But no. Logically speaking, the wine had to come from someone she trusted."

I looked at my hands, and examined my shackles as if with great interest.

"Are you saying she trusted the killer?" he asked me.

"Remember, in her mind, Quickbit was the killer. The other person, X, was shifty, but on her side. At least for the time being. Someone powerful. Someone she had known enough to accept a bottle of wine from, without any second thoughts."

"Oh, *do* cut to the chase, Gates!" Boots banged his fist on the table. "You have our full attention, congratulations. But don't push it, my patience has completely expired now. My term ends tonight, and I *really* look forward to leaving this place as soon as possible."

"I understand, mister mayor, and I promise I'm almost done."

Now that was a bit of a lie. But there was no way I was going to tell the truth by being honest all the time.

The road to hell is paved with good intentions, while the road to heaven is littered with bad decisions gone lucky.

I took out the paper I had found on Redmayne, and slowly unfolded it. You could hear a pin drop. Thankfully, I chose to read it silently first.

You are an idiot, it said.

Even on death's threshold, she was having fun at my expense. I had to improvise once again.

"That person she trusted was you, Mister Mayor."

Time froze. Saul and the barnacle's jaw dropped. Even Nathaniel's eyes went full saucepans.

"Are you..." Boots enunciated slowly, "talking to me?"

"You *are* still the mayor, aren't you?"

Sneer looked like he had missed a few steps on a very dark staircase. Seeing him completely bewildered and at a loss is, to this day, one of my fondest memories.

"Yes, it took me some time to figure this one out. You see, crimes have a clear motive, usually one of two: either robbery, or revenge. I call them the two R's. They are related to the two emotions that will lead people to murder, which are rage and greed. Sadly, I didn't get two other R-words here as well. Close, but no bottle of rum. Like they say, nothing is perfect."

"Why, in God's name, would I want to kill haphazardly people I knew well, right before retiring?" Boots snarled.

Bartholomew was a sight to behold. He had obviously not been trained for that kind of development. His face went through a series of contradictory expressions such as bewilderment, enlightenment, and the dire need to appear in control.

"Well, Mister Mayor, when you put it this way, it does seem absurd. Preposterous some might say. However, and this is crucial, if we proceed to flip things around, the picture starts to make sense."

Boots' eyes were two balls of molten lead that burned me a pair of brand new holes.

"But why, could you ask, why would you want to kill these people, now that retirement was nearby, why, yes indeed, why?"

I was clearly having too much fun with this. But I was gladly willing to pay for it.

"As it is, 'why' would be the wrong question now, wouldn't it? Perhaps, we should try 'how?' As in, 'how does a respected mayor turn into a killer?' And the answer is simple. By making him as broke as a street gambler on Christmas Eve."

"'Why' would have been a perfect fit for that one as well," Nathaniel felt the need to chip in.

"Thank you, duly noted."

I gave him a look. He smiled.

"I hired you," Boots said, his voice shaking. "I, I was the one who hired you, because they said you were good. And now you think that having you unmask me was part of my masterplan?"

He *did* sound convincing. After all, logic and common sense were on his side. But I could see the shift in the audience's attitude. They listened to him, but without sympathy. Not a nod, not even an approving grunt.

Even worse, Bartholomew himself seemed to slowly creep away from his predecessor.

"Considering I was seen as the number one suspect from the get go, anything I could say was instantly disqualified," I said.

"So why did I save your arse the first time? I could have had you locked up as the culprit, then and there, without taking any further unnecessary risk."

"Because it was too early. Quickbit and Redmayne were still alive, and those crimes couldn't have been pinned on me while I was in jail."

"All right, that's enough, this is far beyond ridiculous. What's next? Am I supposed to be Woodes Rogers or Maynard in disguise?"

"Funny you should mention them. Did you know there was a huge ship anchored less than a mile from our shore? I think it was a Man o'War or something. Apologies, I'm a complete ignoramus in these matters. But it was big, with many cannons, and bore the crest of the British crown. Ring any bells?"

The room temperature dropped a few degrees.

"In it, I found goons itching to get us murdered. Oh, and I found *this,* Saul."

I handed him his infamous device that had almost cost me my life during the escape from the ship. I had wrapped it up and kept it with me after leaving Wilbur's boat.

"You found it!" he exclaimed. Then, to the crowd, "he's good."

"Thank you, Saul. But, Mayor Boots, let's come back to why you chose not to comment about your financial difficulties."

"I have nothing to prove, to you, or to anyone in this town. What you are assuming is insane, and a piss-poor attempt to clear yourself of the charges you are obviously guilty of!"

"But is it obvious, really? Strange man comes to town under the pretense of doing police work, starts killing people left and right, only to get caught like a complete idiot?"

"Oh, because 'retiring mayor decides to kill his soon to be ex-citizens' sounds more plausible?"

"If it means that said mayor would find himself generously rewarded for instilling chaos in the fragile free republic of New Cayenne, and then be able to retire comfortably, yes, it does sound more plausible."

Jack Boots became painfully conscious of the way people were looking at him, especially Bartholomew and Selena.

"What? Don't tell me you are going to believe him?"

Their lack of immediate reaction did nothing for his popularity in the room. It was time to go for the kill.

"Not to mention," I added high on my improvising wave, "that *you* were the last person to see Winchester alive, a little fact you had failed to mention during our last meeting. But Lady Winchester saw you, and had to flee. She was hiding, not because she was the culprit, but to avoid becoming the next victim."

Maybe I was going to the gallows, but I wasn't going there alone.

"To verify such an assertion, I call mister Sneer as a witness."

Sneer almost swallowed his Adam's apple. He didn't even think of correcting his name. He just looked embarrassed because of what he was asked to confess.

"This won't be necessary mister Gates," said Bartholomew, "as I will admit to such a meeting."

He put his knuckles on the mayor's desk. Boots looked like a man halfway on a bridge, suddenly realizing that there was in fact no bridge under his feet.

My lucky guess had paid off.

"It was a secret meeting, to discuss political matters that I cannot divulge here. However, when I left, the Admiral was very much alive."

"When *you* left, meaning...?"

He sighed.

"Meaning that being not yet officially in power, I left the mayor and Admiral Winchester for what I supposed was a final goodbye. I never thought it would be *that* final."

The mayor looked like a powder keg that was one spark away from exploding.

"What are you saying man? Have you gone entirely mad?"

He pulled out his sword, with the clear intention of making it go through Bartholomew. The mayor-to-be drew as well, with the ease and confidence of a man holding a gynecologist's tools for the first time.

"*You* went back to kill him!" bellowed Boots.

"I'm afraid you will find out that my skills with these things are quite lacking," answered Bartholomew.

Everyone was suddenly at a loss. No one knew whether to attack the former mayor, or to let him kill what seemed to be an innocent and defenseless man.

I finally found my cutlass, and drew it out. My original idea was more to start a general movement rather than go blade to blade alone against a proper sword. But the Mayor turned to me with the clear intention of skewering me.

"Mayor Gates, I suggest you don't make this situation worse than it already is!" I told him.

"The situation was never bad, at least not for me! But..."

He never finished the sentence. His eyes went blank the second Selena Montgomery broke a splendid Chinese vase on the back of his head. Then he collapsed.

"I'm sorry gentlemen," she said, "but the situation was becoming unacceptably out of hand. You may put away your toys now."

She picked up the two largest shards of the vase.

"Such a shame. I didn't like it very much, but it gave the office some sort of exotic charm."

Chapter 24

"And a bottle for the shantyman"

"You did some interesting intellectual gymnastics there," whispered Nathaniel as he sat down next to me in the mayor's waiting room. We were both rubbing our wrists, appreciating the removal of our chains.

"I wouldn't have had to had I gotten the *assistance* I needed," I scowled.

"I got abducted in the line of duty, mind you," he replied with feigned offense. "And I'm sure it wouldn't have happened had *you* been on time at our rendezvous point."

"Abducted? By whom?"

"By the Town Hall guards."

"Why were the Town Hall guards after you?"

He looked towards the ceiling.

"I may or may have not been lurking around in the cellars."

"Why on earth would you have been doing such a thing?"

"Just a detail, I'll tell you later. How did you end up suspecting Boots?"

"No, this is not *just a detail*."

"Yes, you are right, it is important, and I will tell you all about it. But I need to hear your side first, for mine to make sense. Makes sense?"

I sighed, and spoke:

"Lady Winchester couldn't have done this alone. I witnessed first hand that she was good with swords, but I had a hard time imagining her stabbing her husband. I discovered that Boots owed Winchester a lot of money. It made sense to accuse him. The part about the final meeting was the one thing I needed for my theory to make sense, and so I tried my luck."

"A bluff… I thought you looked odd while saying it."

"Did I?"

"You, my friend, have a very obvious tell."

"Which is?"

"You smile like an idiot. So you thought, since Bart can't hold a sword to save his life, quite literally, it had to be Boots."

"Exactly. Although..." I started musing out loud, but was interrupted by Selena who was peering from behind the office door.

"Gentlemen? Mayor Bartholomew James will see you now."

We got up, and I felt the lack of sleep spill down my knees, and fill my body all the way up to my shoulders.

"Can't we do this a bit later?" whined Nathaniel. "I'm in desperate need of food and deep rest, and I'm not even sure in what order."

She rolled her eyes.

"You're such a spoiled boy. Wait."

She went back in.

"Now your turn," I said. "What were you doing in the cellars?"

"While you were on your way to woo Redmayne, I decided to go back to Drake's End."

"Instead of…"

"Instead of following your bad idea. I had no business going to Town Hall. You had missed some important things, do you know that?"

"I'm sorry, I was under the impression you were with me that first time, weren't you?"

"Great leaders give credit when it's due, and take full responsibility in case of defeat."

"I'm not defeated!"

"And it'll be thanks to me."

"What's that amazing thing you found?"

The door reopened.

"Mayor James invites you to eat with him, as he himself is about to have a quick bite before taking up his duties."

"From what they say," Nathaniel nudged me in the ribs, "the cook over here is to die for. Don't know if it's in a good way, but I'm definitely curious. You?"

"Very well," I said. "Let's have a celebratory bite. Then it's off to bed."

We walked in to find the new mayor sitting next to a window. He was looking out towards the horizon, his shirt undone, and his sleeves rolled up.

"Looks like you could do with a bit of shut-eye, Mister Mayor," I told him.

"I like the expression," he replied. "Indeed, it has been a trying couple of days."

"Did you at any point suspect him?" I continued.

He let out a heavy sigh. Then he rubbed his forehead, and looked at me.

"In these cases, you end up suspecting everyone. When you've been in as many trials as I've been, you begin to develop a certain knack for these things. Don't take this the wrong way, but I also seriously suspected you."

"As you should have, Mister Mayor, as you should have."

Nathaniel rolled his eyes.

"Anyways, I'm having a few cold cuts, if you care to join me. May even have some wine or ale to wash it down, if there's any of it left."

"In my position, and with my salary, it would be idiotic to refuse a free meal."

Bartholomew laughed.

"I'm sorry things had to start this way. Please gentlemen, take a seat."

He stood up, and took glasses off a high shelf.

"I've always wanted to try those. Mayor Boots kept them for a special occasion, and I believe it's safe to say that this qualifies as one."

"It helps when you're *that* tall" I noticed.

Nathaniel, Selena, and I sat down on nearby chairs, while Bartholomew dragged a round coffee table in our midst.

"I'll get the food, and *will* take offense if any of you tries to help."

He left.

"Not too bad for a new mayor," Nathaniel said.

"It wears off very quickly, trust me," Selena said. "The position sadly doth make or rather unmake the man."

Outside, merchants were shouting about the quality of their goods, while customers were shouting back their doubts about the quality of their goods. Life on the docks was going on, oblivious to the little drama that had just unfolded.

Bartholomew came back with two trays, and a keg of ale under his armpit.

"Found these, thought it would be a shame to let them go to waste. With the incoming crisis, it'll be a long time before we can get our hands on such delicacies."

He set the trays on the coffee table, and the keg next to us.

"I do apologize if I treat myself to a bit of wine, but I've been eyeing these bottles for a while."

He reached behind the mayor's desk, and brought out a bottle. I felt my eyes bulge when I recognized the label.

But before I could say anything, Nathaniel bumped his knee into mine, and gave me a look. Either he was going for a repeat of the cemetery scene, or he was trying to tell me something.

The wine. He was trying to tell me something about the wine. He knew about it. And he wanted me to shut up.

I decided to trust him, so I played along.

"If it's all the same to you, Mister Mayor," Nathaniel said, "I wouldn't mind joining you with a cup of wine".

"Sure, that would be my pleasure. Nothing like a red wine to compliment cold cuts."

"Count me in as well," Selena said, "but just a bit, we still have work to do."

Nathaniel took the bottle, looked at it like a connoisseur, and filled our glasses. He gave me a sharp look, almost commanding.

"I guess I'll save the beer for later," I said. "No use in being antisocial all the time."

I raised my glass, and Nathaniel poured me a generous portion.

"A toast," declared Bartholomew, "to the future of New Cayenne."

I looked at Nate, waiting for a signal to stop pretending, and avoid drinking. But to my horror, he downed his glass in the most indecent fashion. I was so shocked that I forgot to prevent Selena from swallowing a more acceptable sip.

Had I missed something? Was the plan to commit mass suicide in order to bring a clean end to this case?

Nathaniel pinched his lips while looking at my drink, and I had a small epiphany. Maybe I could afford to trust him.

"To testing theories," I said.

It actually tasted good.

At that point, Bartholomew went into a coughing fit that almost threw him on the floor.

"Oh my God, Mister Mayor!" shouted Selena.

Nathaniel looked puzzled.

"You're not supposed to look puzzled!" I told him.

He raised his hand to shut me up. Selena caught up faster than me, and just frowned at Nate.

Bartholomew James' cough ended almost as quickly as it started. He stood up, cleared his throat, and looked at us, one after the other.

"I'm sorry, I have some issues with red wine."

He picked up his untouched glass, and twirled it into the sunlight coming in from the window.

"You see, this vintage was tampered with to make it more... Useful."

I slapped my forehead.

"Of course! Of course, what a complete and utter idiot! Nate!"

"Yes Chas, I know."

"No, but the other person, during the secret cemetery meeting. He said 'you pirates'. '*You* pirates' Nate."

"Already there Chas."

"Means the culprit was not a pirate!"

I turned around, and pointed at Bartholomew.

"And of course," I said. "Yes! Of course, you're the one who poisoned Steve!"

Bartholomew looked at me with a shimmer of panic in his eyes.

"After that meeting with Redmayne, you escaped in the jungle, and ran into the local crocodile."

"Caiman," corrected Nathaniel.

"Not important, Nate. And you tried to kill him with a flask of arsenic, but it did nothing. *That's* why he fell asleep when I threw him my bottle! The mix made him slumber, poor thing. And of course, it all makes sense, silly me. You are a tall man as well, tall enough to get these glasses, and tall enough to grab the decorative swords in Winchester's waiting room. And to hang Quickbit without a stool. Oh my God, you were hiding there with Redmayne as well! Fancy that! We were all there together, playing hide and seek!"

Bartholomew did not seem amused.

"And yes, of course you would use poison. The only adversary you can stab is a dead one. That's why the poison, *then* the stabbing. To think that Wilbur took you for a woman because of the well-groomed hair."

"Probably also the manicured hands," added Nathaniel.

"Yes, good point."

Bartholomew stood up.

"I'm sorry to say that you're a bit late for that. You all have but less than a few minutes to live. This little puny republic of yours will die, and civilization under the crown will continue its flawless path to greatness."

"What?" shouted Selena, grabbing her throat. "You miserable weasel, it was you?" She turned to me. "And you accused poor Jack? When he was innocent?"

"You came close," Bartholomew said to me. "You just bet on the wrong mayor."

"I guess I did. It makes more sense actually. *You're* the agent sent by Woodes Rogers."

Finally, some satisfaction. I hated accusing poor old Boots.

Then, panic.

"But how did you plan to keep Lady Winchester silent? Surely she knows the truth?"

"The prisoners are given wine with their meals, you know, an old pirate tradition," Bartholomew said. "You'll all end up in the same… Boat."

We all waited, Nathaniel looking smug, me listening closely to my belly's whims and growls, and Selena waiting in agony for the poison to do its job.

"I really hope you succeeded at what you planned to do," I told Nathaniel.

"Well I still hear you nagging, don't I? Surely it must be a good sign?"

Bartholomew had lost all his sense of humor. He narrowed his eyes.

"You little bastard," he spat at Nathaniel, "I knew I should have double checked the wine."

"Good thinking, Nate", I nodded, "good thinking."

"Someone please fill me in," cried out Selena.

"I had found a bottle of wine at Drake's End," he told her, "that had probably rolled in a dark corner. A bottle that looked somehow familiar, and that smelled way too acid to be wine. I came back here, as quietly as possible, and found crates of that same wine in the cellars, with the same odd smell. Struck by the beginning of a good idea, something Chas wouldn't know about…"

"To the point Nate."

"Getting there. So what I did was replace the contents of these bottles with what seemed like honest wine from the old barrels. If someone was poisoning people, it seemed like a good way to figure out who was doing it."

"Does that mean we are not dying?" asked Selena.

"Oh I wouldn't go that far!" Bartholomew said.

He had grabbed his sword from the desk, unsheathed it, and drew a gun.

"Are you as good a shooter as you are a swordsman?" asked Nathaniel. "Because if that's the case, I suggest you just put them down before you hurt yourself."

Without flinching, Bartholomew aimed at Nathaniel, and shot before anyone could react.

The bang deafened us, and threw poor Nate on the floor.

"I guess I can shoot after all," the mayor said.

I took my cutlass out. The man was perhaps a lousy fighter, but he was quick. I had to do as much damage as possible before he did. He read my thoughts, or followed the same logic, because before I even managed to raise my blade to strike, he threw his pistol at my wrist.

There was a snap, like the breaking of a twig. And pain, a white flashing pain that shot from my hand all the way to my forehead.

He threw himself at me, the pointy end of his sword going for my chest. I was too stunned to react.

"Move, you idiot!" Selena shouted as she shoved me away from Bartholomew's blow.

He missed me by an inch. I stumbled on Nathaniel's unconscious body.

I immediately looked up. If she had pushed me out of harm's way, it meant she had stepped right into it.

"I hope you're not planning on making this a habit," she said.

As it turns out, she had kicked Bartholomew's sword out of his hand without breaking a sweat.

"If you plan on letting me clean up all your messes you've got another thing coming. I have developed a serious headache from dealing with these two for the past week."

As Bartholomew bent down to retrieve his blade, she drew hers and placed it under his throat.

"Wait! Don't kill him!" I shouted.

The man froze, and winced preventively as she pushed the blade's edge against his jugular.

"What? You're not *entirely* sure it's him?" she asked, exasperated.

"No, I mean yes, but we still need him to know who he worked with!"

"Oh good grief!"

The hilt of her sword casually landed on the back of his head. He fell down like a very tall sack of potatoes.

I examined Nathaniel.

The bullet had hit him in the stomach.

Bartholomew's gun yielded enough firepower to kill a bull, which reduced Nate's chances of survival to a little under zero.

"You annoying idiot, should have run away when you had the chance, like you promised," I said, pulling his shirt up to fully assess the damage.

I found nothing. I pulled the shirt higher, wondering about the flexibility of his anatomy.

"Chas, we're not there yet you naughty boy," Nathaniel said.

"Where were you actually hit?" I asked him.

Out of his shirt, he pulled a book. *The* book. The bullet had dug itself halfway through its pages.

"Another Saint Teach miracle," Nathaniel said. "Still think it was a bad idea to steal it?"

"How does it keep ending up in your possession?"

"It's too good to let go, Chas, too good to let go."

"I suppose there *is* a God for annoying idiots," said Selena. "Congratulations Gates, you get to keep yours. I hope it's for the best."

Chapter 25

"And here's to the health of each true hearted lass"

Boots had finally opened his eyes. But after a few seconds of readjusting to reality, he noticed me next to his bed, and squinted in a way that would have made a mountain gorilla nervous.
"Hello Mister Mayor! Glad to see you safe and sound."
"My innocence will be proven, you miserable prawn, and you will find yourself in one hell of a-"
"About that, sorry to interrupt you, but you are no longer accused of anything. All cleared. With my sincerest apologies, of course."
At that point, Nathaniel burst in the room, panting.
"Hey is he...? Mayor Boots, you're back!"
Boots' stare was burning with all the fires of hell.
"Right," Nate said, "so, no hard feelings?"
"You," Boots started, managing to turn a single syllable into two ("ee-yoo"). "You have no idea of the amount of retribution I am capable of."
He chewed each word, like a bloodhound mauling its prey.
"Jack," I squeezed myself back in the conversation, "I know how bad it looked, but it is part of the process. Thanks to this, we were able to arrest Bartholomew James. And this time, without a single doubt."

He struggled to sit up, and we jumped in to assist him.

"Away! Stay away you parasites!" he swatted us. "You can't *begin* to imagine the amount of damage you have done!"

"Glad to see the mayor at the top of his shape," Nathaniel said, "I'll leave you two sort out the details. Toodle-oo!"

He left without bothering to close the door.

"Mister Mayor, I really need you to wait for me to finish explaining. It will be better for your heart, and your general well-being."

"Ha, I'll show you my well-being all right!"

"Oh enough!" I shouted. "I understand how angry and bewildered you must feel, but you will eventually have to get over yourself. And what's that supposed to mean 'I'll show you my well-being'? You're going to look fresh and healthy while you beat me to a pulp? I was this close to being hanged, let's have some perspective over here, shall we?"

He was taken aback. To be honest, even I was surprised by my outburst.

"That's how cases are solved," I continued before he could escalate again. "You test a few theories, ruffle a few feathers, instigate chaos, and only then, can the answers come up."

He relaxed, but the loathing remained in his glare.

"Do I have to expect being accused of the worst every time you have a case?" he asked.

"I'll be sure to pass the blame around as much as possible."

He gave this some consideration, then stretched, and scratched his head. I had to stifle a yawn.

"So, Bartholomew?" he finally said.

"It seems so."

"Drat. Who's going to replace me now?"

"Not him, I guess."

"No... I have to organize his hanging, pain in the ass..."
"Then, let's not do it."
"Don't be daft, I can't let a murderer walk free."
"The thing is, he might still be useful. Kept in a cell, he could even become an asset."
"The man has killed three times."
"Technically, two at the moment."
"You still have hopes for Redmayne?"
"I haven't heard anything from the alchemists yet."
He stared at his lap.
"But he's still a killer."
"A killer linked to a very long chain of command entirely dedicated to our destruction. He is more useful in jail than at the end of a rope."
"Your naivete is impressive. Do you really see him helping us?"
"I just need you to trust me on this. If need be, sentence him to the gallows, but have the execution delayed. Please."
He threw away his blanket, and stood up. His balance was still a bit off, like that of a tightrope walker in a strong wind.
"Shouldn't you be resting a bit more?" I suggested.
"And let you run the show? After today's performance, I'm not sure if I'll ever be able to sleep properly again. No, I better get back to work, and in the meantime, you can go check on Captain Redmayne."
I may have blushed. Boots smirked and acted as if he hadn't noticed, but I definitely felt my face warm up. I stammered, trying to come up with something casual to say. Then I remembered that Clarisse Redmayne was very close to death, which sobered me up.

"Very well, Mister Mayor. I know it's not a mutual feeling, but I am looking forward to working a bit longer with you."
"I'm sure it will be anything but boring."

Chapter 26
Pirates don't die, they fade into legend

The ride to Reine and Félix was not as smooth as the previous one. Sally had been kind to me in my darkest moment, but it was time to remind everyone who the real master was. This was not lost on the townspeople, who would certainly make sure to add this story to the local folklore. "How Charles Gates Went Riding Through Town, Holding On to His Mare's Tail While Sitting Backwards" would be the highlight of many a drunken night at the Sinking Squid.

I climbed up the stairs to the shop a bit quicker than I expected. All I could think of was how long it had taken me to get there with Clarisse. I had given the poison too much time to creep inside her system. Had her body still been limp when I reached Reine and Félix? Or had it begun to grow a bit stiff?

Before I knew it, I was banging on the door once again.

"Don't you know how to knock like a proper human being?" Reine asked as she opened.

"Apologies, I promise I'll be able to as soon as all of this is over." Her face seemed gaunt.

"You don't have good news for me, do you?" I asked.

She gestured me in, and closed the door.

"Who did this to her?" she asked.
"Bartholomew. James. Bartholomew James. The new mayor."
"Oh, that very tall, wiry man? Boots' replacement?"
"The very man."
I could feel my heart sinking.
"Did she suffer?"
"Quite a lot. When you brought her in, the arsenic had taken over. There was very little life left in her. Too little."
I had reached the very deep end of my endurance. I just sat on the floor, back to the wall, and let my head hang. I felt completely drained, with a big lump in my chest.
"She has lost the use of her left leg. It's too early to say if she will fully regain her mental capacities. We have flushed out the poison as much as we could, but there will be some irreversible damage."
I looked at her.
"Are you saying... That she's still alive?"
"Of course she's still alive! Oh, you had thought…"
Her eyes were stern, but her lips hinted at a smile.
"She still needs to rest, though. Félix brought her back home. But I'm glad to see your interest in her was a bit more than just professional."
I looked down and cleared my throat.
"Ha, you won me my bet! Félix will be glad to know that he got himself a whole month of cleaning the jars of expired medicine. And boy, do these get to smell nasty."
I finally managed to smile.

Chapter 27

"Haul away your anchor"

I gave Sally a pat on the muzzle.
"All right girl, I'm giving you the rest of the day off. I'll walk."
She let out a sound that was halfway between a snort and a sigh, then returned the cuddle.
"I promise, you'll get other chances to catapult me into the ether."
Although I was well beyond exhausted, I chose the long way back home. Partly because I took a few wrong turns, but also because I enjoyed getting to see the town without the looming threat of being arrested and put to death.
Reine had loaned me a long brown leather coat that had seen its fair share of storms and scorching suns. But it did the job of hiding the traces of my encounter with Steve.
As a result, I did not get that many stares, and managed to enjoy a bit of anonymity in the colorful crowd that filled the uneven streets of New Cayenne.
The very second I stepped inside my headquarters, my body went limp. I needed a bed, and hopefully mine had some sort of mattress and a blanket. A pillow was probably too much to ask for.
"Well look who's finally back," said Nathaniel, his two feet crossed on the front desk. "Welcome to the P.P.H.Q.!"

"Too tired to argue. Now if you'll excuse me, I still have to discover what my bedroom looks like."

He grimaced.

"If I were you, I'd keep my expectations as low as possible."

"Yes, I was planning to."

I made my way to the staircase.

"Before you pass out, the mayor wants you to know that you must write something about this case."

"Ugh, paperwork. I thought I had left that behind in Bristol."

"The world is changing Chas, and pirates have to follow or perish."

"I'll solve that dilemma when I regain some lucidity. Anything else?"

"Two things. Lady Winchester would like to have a word with you."

"I'm sure she does, but I'm afraid she'll have to wait. What else?"

"I left you a little something on your bed. Some kind of welcome gift."

"Really? Weren't you planning on vanishing as soon as you had the chance?"

"Oh I will. Just waiting for the proper opportunity. Sleep tight!"

I climbed up the stairs, and found my room.

The bed was an actual bed. The blue paint on its wooden planks had been peeling off it for a while, but it stood on its four feet. The mattress was filled with feathers, some of them sneaking out. There was a thick brown blanket made of wool, with surprisingly not too many holes.

And there was a pillow.

My exhaustion blossomed to its fullest, and I just collapsed, barely noticing the view from the window of the town's rooftops. I would have the rest of my life to admire it through rested eyes.

And that's when it hit me. Or rather, I hit it.

As my body made contact with the gentle softness of the bed, something sharp went up my side, sending a flash of exquisite pain up my spine.

Too weak to scream, I groaned. Angrily.

I hadn't noticed a darker patch of brown on the blanket. A darker, thick patch, with pointy angles.

I pulled it out from under me, and saw I had guessed right.

Nathaniel's welcome gift. The cookbook. Blackbeard's bloody cookbook. Complete with the bullet.

"You will be the death of me," I said to it.

The End

Epilogue

It smelled of humidity down there. The cold wet stones were heavy with the sea that tried to move in.

There weren't many cells in the Town Hall basement, but they gave Bartholomew a decent one: it had a bench.

The man sat on it, his legs crossed, as if awaiting an important meeting. He wasn't going anywhere of course, but letting himself go was just not who he was.

He lifted his head, and had a start.

"I didn't hear you arrive."

"Apologies, I did all I could not to disturb your precious train of thoughts.'

"Didn't I kill you?"

"No, it seems not. Can't win them all, right?"

Bartholomew sighed, and bowed his head.

"Are you here for a well-deserved revenge?"

"Revenge may happen along the way, but later on the menu. Right now, I need to see if you can be of any use."

"I suppose you know you won't get anything from me?"

"Of course, of course, it goes without saying. I don't expect you to betray anyone. I'm more interested in you helping *me* betray someone."

Bartholomew couldn't help looking back at him. He hadn't expected this.

"Is this a trap?"

"I don't know how to put this, but you're *already* trapped. And on your way to be hanged."

"Isn't it hung?"

"Oh don't start as well. Do you want a way out or not?"

The prisoner smirked.

"What would the price be?"

"Just your cooperation, Mister James. In due time, of course."

Nathaniel smiled.

About the author

J.L.Henry lives in Oslo, Norway, with his wife and three children. He believes he makes the best burgers in the world, and all his imaginary friends agree.

Find him on www.JamesLouisHenry.com, and on J.L.HenryAuthor on Facebook, Instagram and TikTok, for updates, discussions about the books, and recipes about burgers.

Acknowledgments

A big thank you to the Facebook page Shipwrecked with Captain Marrow, for the pirate history, the beautiful pictures, and the inspiration to move forward with my stories.

Thank you to Chris Rowan for turning my blurb into a damn good one. Like Verrocchio said about Leonardo da Vinci, there are those who know, and those who know nothing.

Thank you to Melody Pate for catching what twenty-three rewrites didn't. You are a writer's guardian angel.

And last but not least thank you to my wife for bringing my characters to life with her take on them. I now feel I could actually meet them on the bus (which would freak me out but in an awesome way).

Printed in Great Britain
by Amazon